ORNAMENTS GALORE Volume 2

Ursula Michael's *Ornaments Galore* cross stitch pattern book has been so well-received that we are elated to present *Ornaments Galore, Volume 2*! This second collection of Christmas designs includes cheerful elves, bears, birds, angels, reindeer, Santas—48 festive images to brighten your holidays. Use these little creations to trim the tree, or tie them to packages for cheery presentations. They're also perfect for ornament exchanges or secret pal surprises! To get the Leisure Arts book that started it all, #3980 *Ornaments Galore*, visit your local retailer or www.leisurearts.com. Dozens of fun holiday ornaments are just stitches away!

MEET Ursula Michael

Ursula Michael has always loved to sew, paint, and draw. She trained at the Paier College of Art in New Haven, Connecticut. After working several years as a graphic artist, she discovered there was a market for original needlework patterns. Before long, she was selling designs to a variety of publishers and creating her own line of cross stitch kits and patterns.

When she moved from Connecticut to Rhode Island, Ursula began to focus entirely on design work, producing about 200 new designs per year! She filled her workspace with fabric, thread, books, and art materials. In this colorful atmosphere,Ursula currently divides her work hours between her computer, sewing machine, and antique drafting table.

But she also finds time for another important element of life—fun.

"My dog Maverick keeps me company in the studio, which overlooks an ocean bay," she says. "We go for walks and listen to jazz music. And when no one is watching, I sometimes dance to Jimmy Buffet!"

When asked what she likes best about designing needlework, Ursula says, "It's my goal to make the stitcher smile while she works on one of my designs. And I hope that when the same design is finished, it brings joy to whoever sees it."

If you would like to view more of Ursula's joyful artistry and catch up on what she's doing now, visit www.UrsulaMichael.com.

LEISURE ARTS, INC.
Maumelle, Arkansas

8

9

10

11

12

12

13

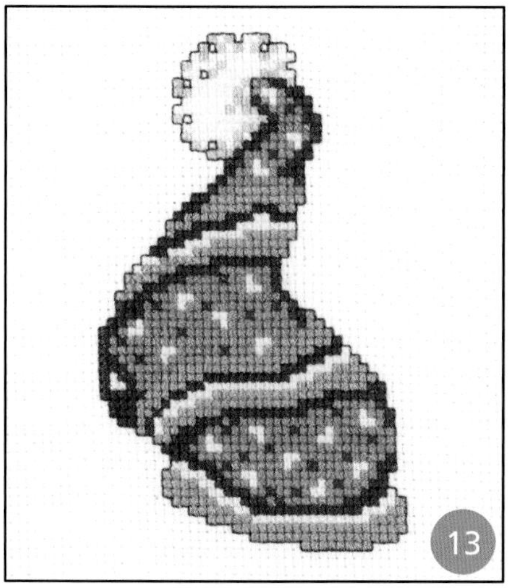
13

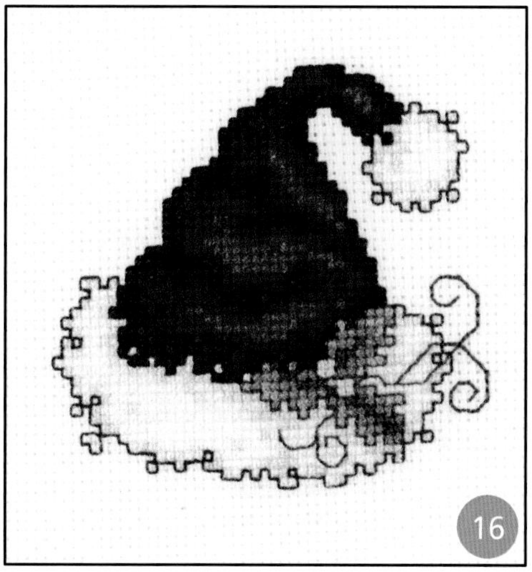
16

15

16

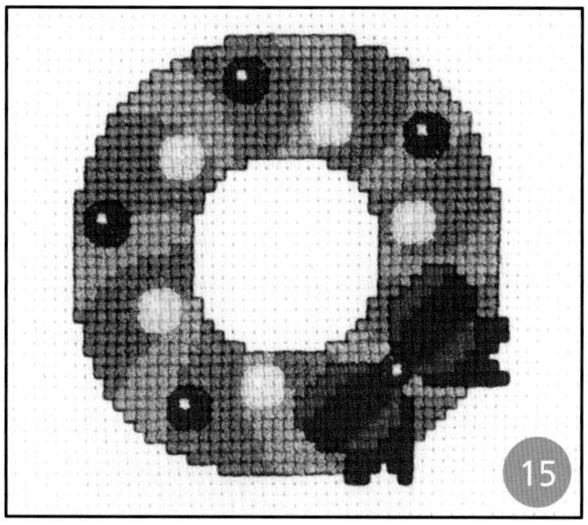
15

7

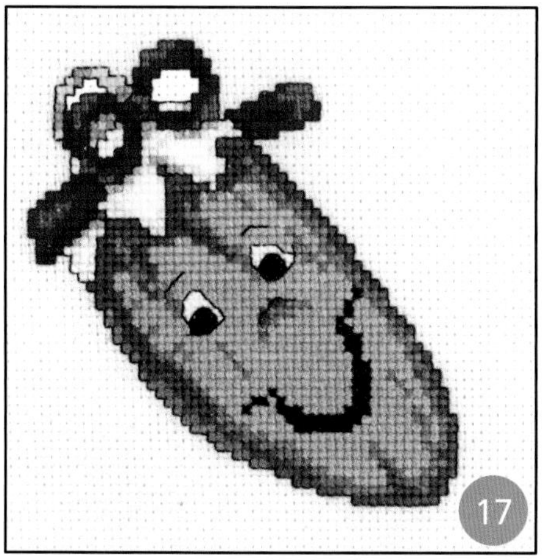
17

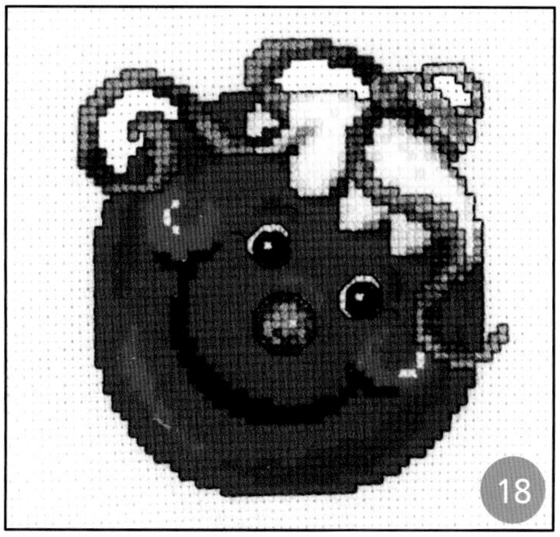
18

19

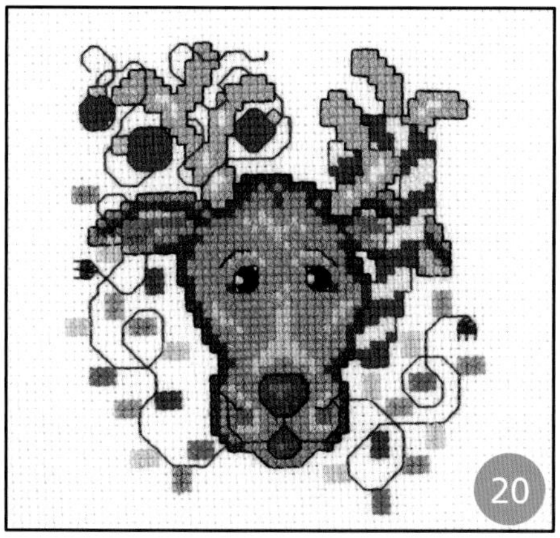
20

2010
46

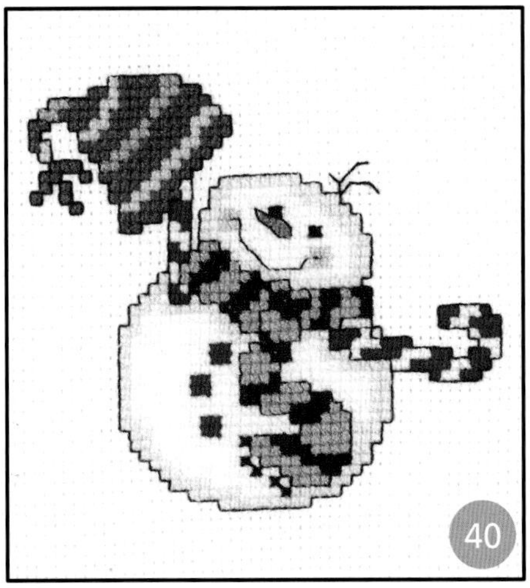
40

40

43

41

44

43

45

39

42

32

31

33

14

14

38

36

37

42

21

22

23

26

25

24

27

28

29

34

30

35

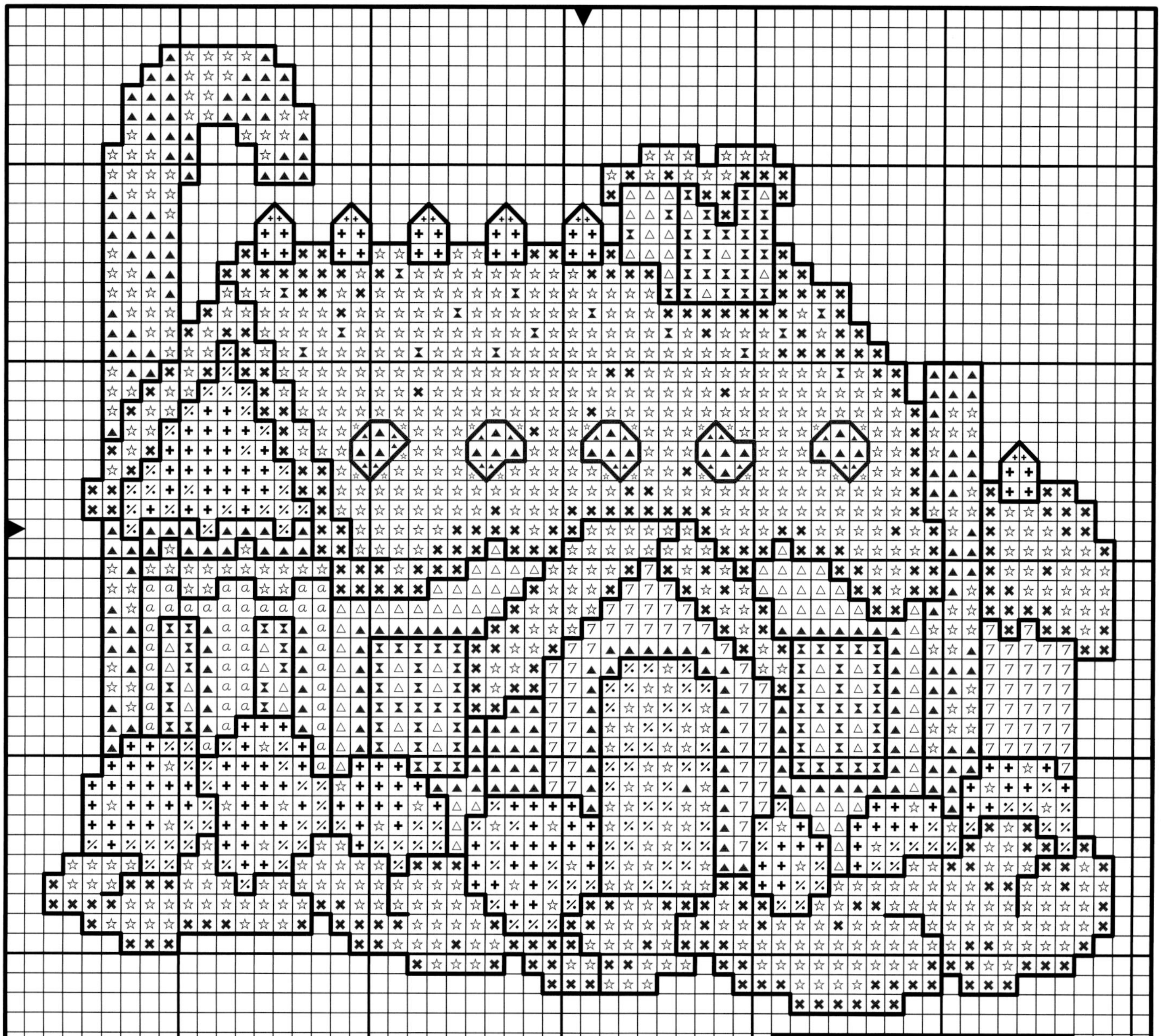

Stitch Count (56w x 49h)	
14 count	4" x $3^1/_2$"
16 count	$3^1/_2$" x $3^1/_8$"
18 count	$3^1/_8$" x $2^3/_4$"

GINGERBREAD HOUSE

X	DMC	$^1/_4$X	B'ST	ANC.	COLOR
☆	blanc	☆		2	white
	310		/	403	black
▲	321	▲	/	9046	red
✖	415			398	lt grey
⧗	434			310	brown
△	436			1045	tan
⁒	701			227	green
+	703	+		238	lt green
a	738			361	lt tan
7	3705			35	melon

Design was stitched on an 8" x $7^1/_2$" piece of 14 count white Aida (design size 4" x $3^1/_2$"). Three strands of floss were used for Cross Stitch and 1 strand for Backstitch.

Shown on page 3.

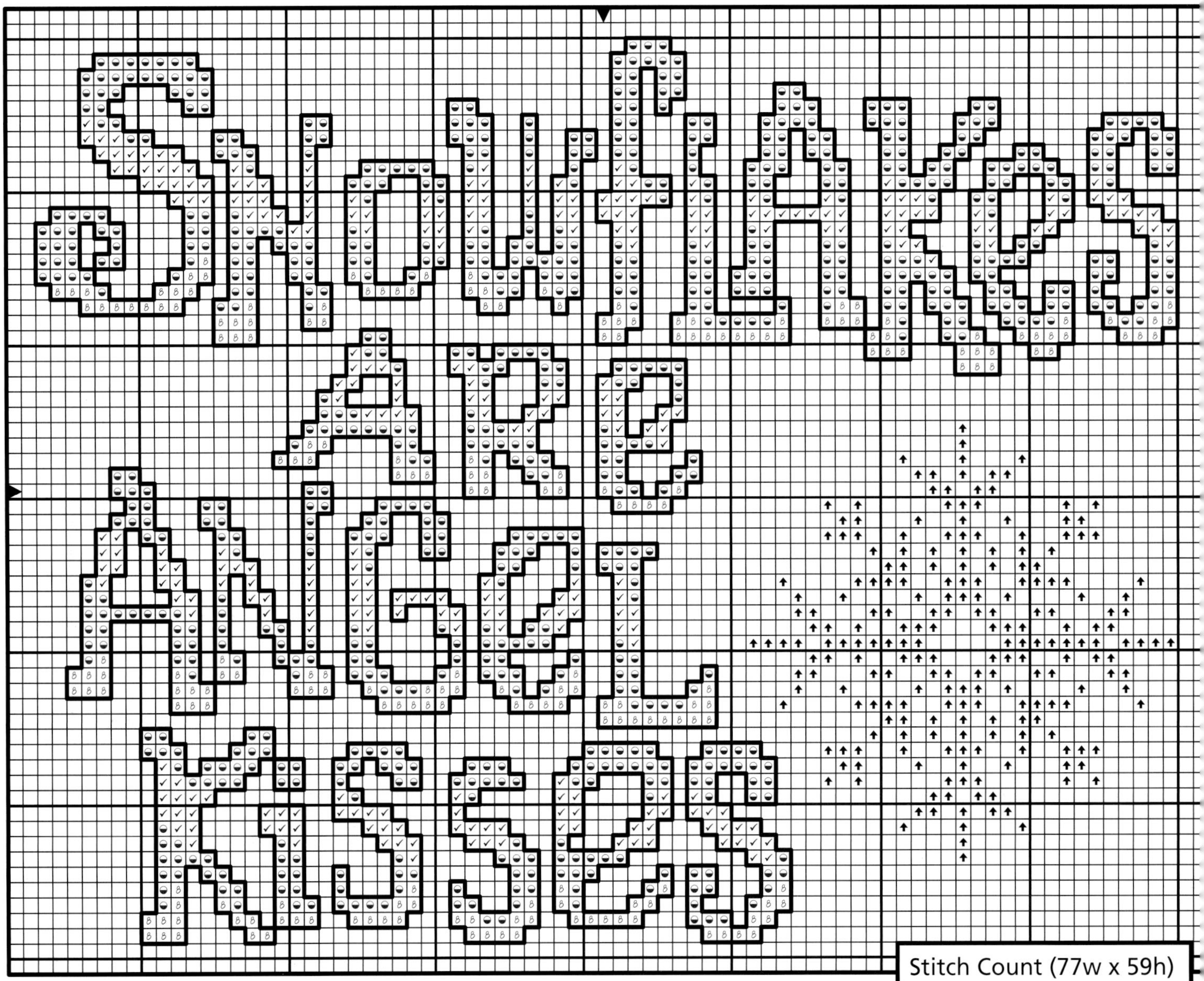

Stitch Count (77w x 59h)

14 count	$5^1/_2$" x $4^1/_4$"
16 count	$4^7/_8$" x $3^3/_4$"
18 count	$4^3/_8$" x $3^3/_8$"

ANGEL KISSES

X	DMC	B'ST	ANC.	COLOR
8	797	/	132	dk blue
◒	799		136	blue
✓	800		144	lt blue
↑	995		410	turquoise

Design was stitched on a $9^1/_2$" x $8^1/_2$" piece of 14 count white Aida (design size $5^1/_2$" x $4^1/_4$"). Three strands of floss were used for Cross Stitch and 1 strand for Backstitch.

Shown on page 2.

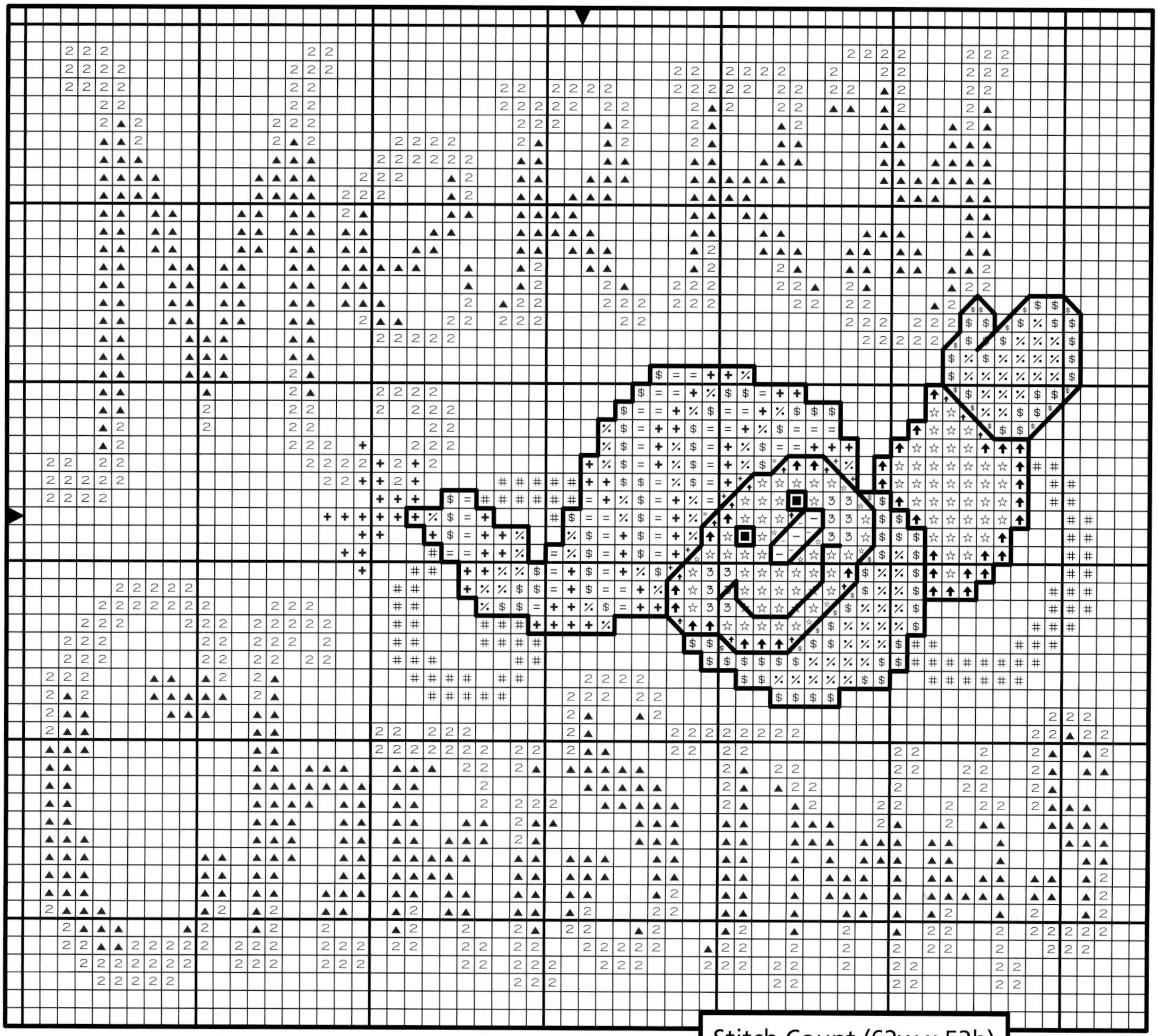

Stitch Count (62w x 53h)

14 count	$4^1/_2$" x $3^7/_8$"
16 count	$3^7/_8$" x $3^3/_8$"
18 count	$3^1/_2$" x 3"

MERRY CHRISTMAS

X	DMC	$^1/_4$X	B'ST	ANC.	COLOR
☆	blanc	◺☆		2	white
■	310		╱	403	black
▲	321			9046	red
3	353			6	peach
$	699	◺$		923	dk green
⁒	701			227	green
+	703	◺+		238	lt green
=	726	◺=		295	yellow
⬆	762	◺⬆		234	lt grey
#	809			130	blue
2	816			1005	maroon
−	970	◺−		316	orange

Design was stitched on an $8^1/_2$" x 8" piece of 14 count white Aida (design size $4^1/_2$" x $3^7/_8$"). Three strands of floss were used for Cross Stitch and 1 strand for Backstitch.

Shown on page 2.

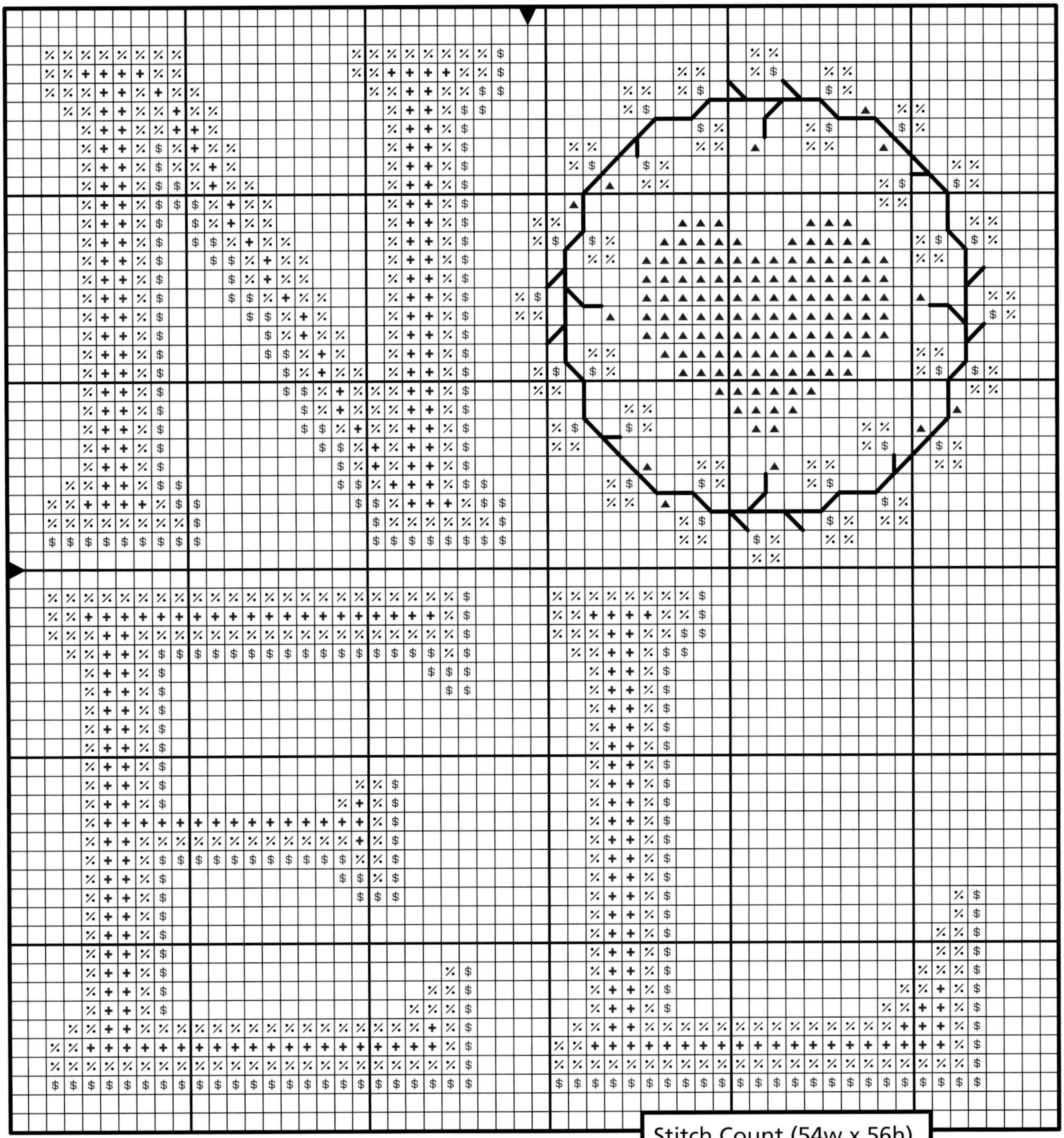

Stitch Count (54w x 56h)	
14 count	$3^7/_8$" x 4"
16 count	$3^3/_8$" x $3^1/_2$"
18 count	3" x $3^1/_8$"

NOEL

X	DMC	B'ST	ANC.	COLOR
▲	321		9046	red
$	699		923	dk green
⁒	701	/	227	green
+	703		238	lt green

Design was stitched on an 8" x 8" piece of 14 count white Aida (design size $3^7/_8$" x 4"). Three strands of floss were used for Cross Stitch and 1 strand for Backstitch.

Shown on page 2.

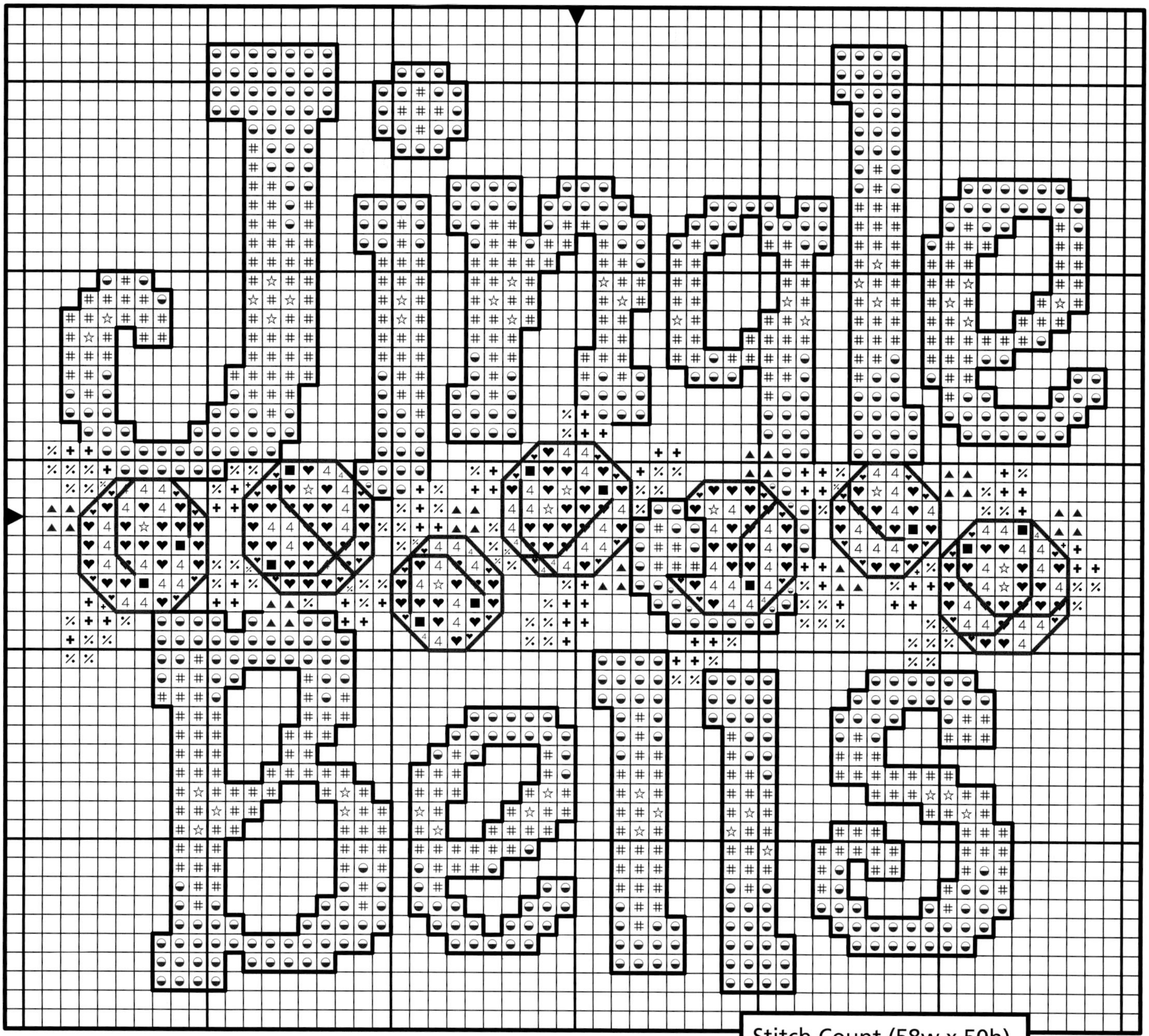

Stitch Count (58w x 50h)	
14 count	$4^{1}/_{4}$" x $3^{5}/_{8}$"
16 count	$3^{5}/_{8}$" x $3^{1}/_{8}$"
18 count	$3^{1}/_{4}$" x $2^{7}/_{8}$"

JINGLE BELLS

X	DMC	1/4X	B'ST	ANC.	COLOR
☆	blanc			2	white
■	310		/	403	black
▲	321			9046	red
⁒	701	◺⁒		227	green
+	703	◺+		238	lt green
♥	726	◺♥		295	yellow
	797		/	132	dk blue
◒	799	◺◒		136	lt blue
#	809			130	blue
4	3852	◺4		306	gold

Design was stitched on an $8^{1}/_{2}$" x 8" piece of 14 count white Aida (design size $4^{1}/_{4}$" x $3^{5}/_{8}$"). Three strands of floss were used for Cross Stitch and 1 strand for Backstitch.

Shown on page 2.

Stitch Count (34w x 50h)	
14 count	$2^1/_2$" x $3^5/_8$"
16 count	$2^1/_8$" x $3^1/_8$"
18 count	2" x $2^7/_8$"

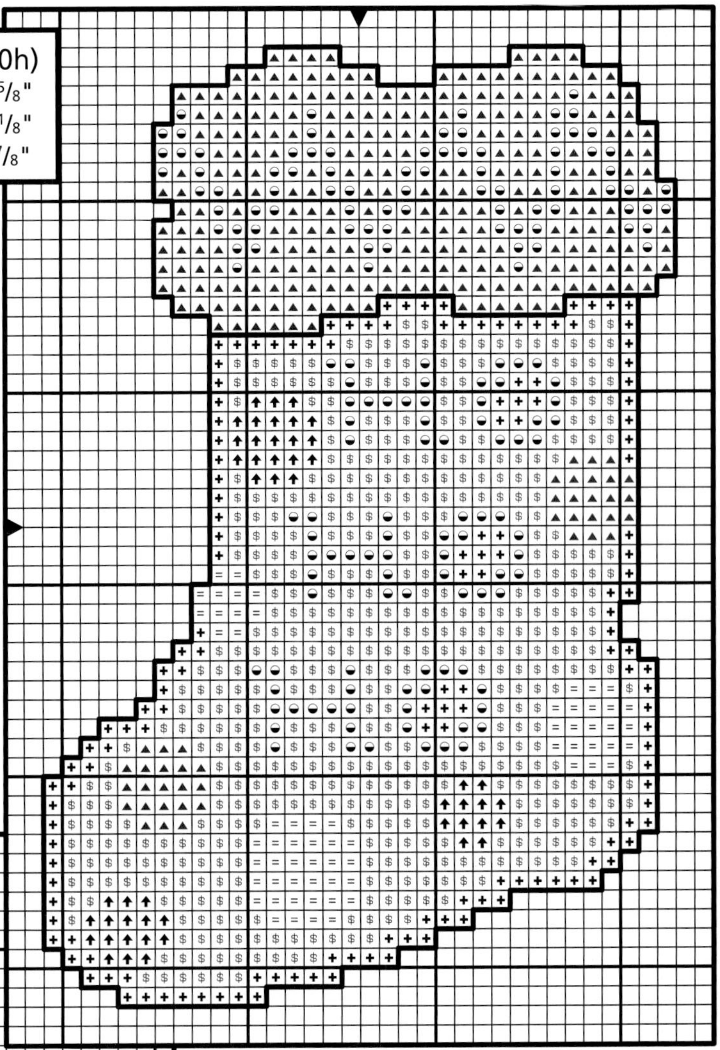

HO HO HO STOCKING

X	DMC	B'ST	ANC.	COLOR
◒	blanc		2	white
	310	/	403	black
▲	321		9046	red
$	699		923	dk green
+	703		238	green
=	726		295	yellow
⬆	995		410	turquoise

Design was stitched on a $6^1/_2$" x 8" piece of 14 count white Aida (design size $2^1/_2$" x $3^5/_8$"). Three strands of floss were used for Cross Stitch and 1 strand for Backstitch.

Shown on page 2.

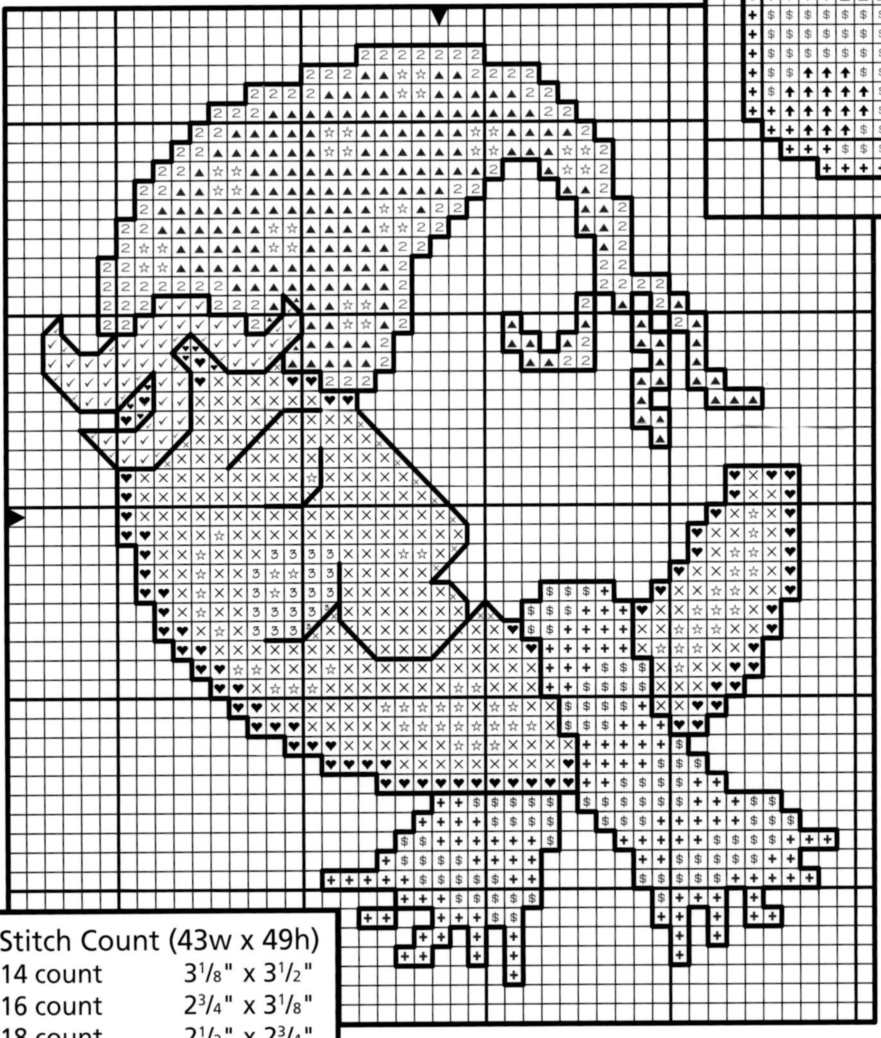

Stitch Count (43w x 49h)	
14 count	$3^1/_8$" x $3^1/_2$"
16 count	$2^3/_4$" x $3^1/_8$"
18 count	$2^1/_2$" x $2^3/_4$"

MAN IN MOON

X	DMC	1/4X	B'ST	ANC.	COLOR
☆	blanc			2	white
	310		/	403	black
♥	318	◩		399	grey
▲	321	◩		9046	red
3	353			6	peach
$	699			923	dk green
+	703			238	green
×	762	◩		234	lt grey
✓	800	◩		144	lt blue
2	816			1005	maroon

Design was stitched on a $7^1/_2$" x $7^1/_2$" piece of 14 count white Aida (design size $3^1/_8$" x $3^1/_2$"). Three strands of floss were used for Cross Stitch and 1 strand for Backstitch.

Shown on page 2.

JOY STOCKING

X	DMC	B'ST	ANC.	COLOR
☆	blanc		2	white
	310	╱	403	black
▲	321		9046	red
$	699		923	dk green
+	703		238	green
=	726		295	yellow
✖	797		132	dk blue
♥	816		1005	dk red

Design was stitched on a 6½" x 8" piece of 14 count white Aida (design size 2½" x 3⅝"). Three strands of floss were used for Cross Stitch and 1 strand for Backstitch.

Shown on page 2.

Stitch Count (34w x 50h)	
14 count	2½" x 3⅝"
16 count	2⅛" x 3⅛"
18 count	2" x 2⅞"

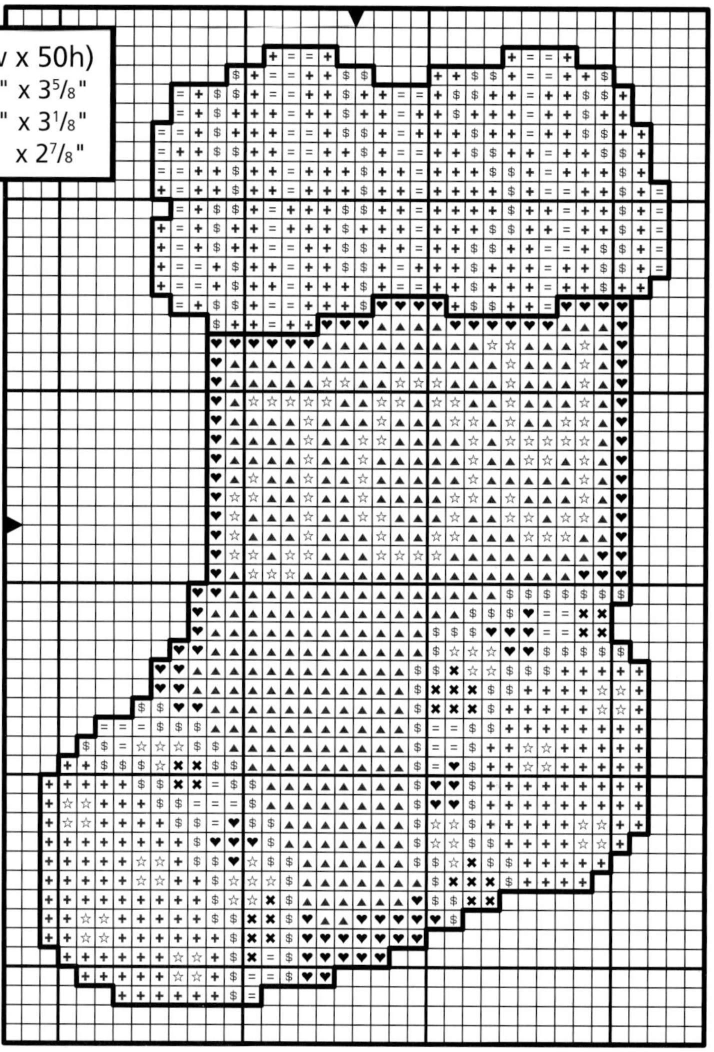

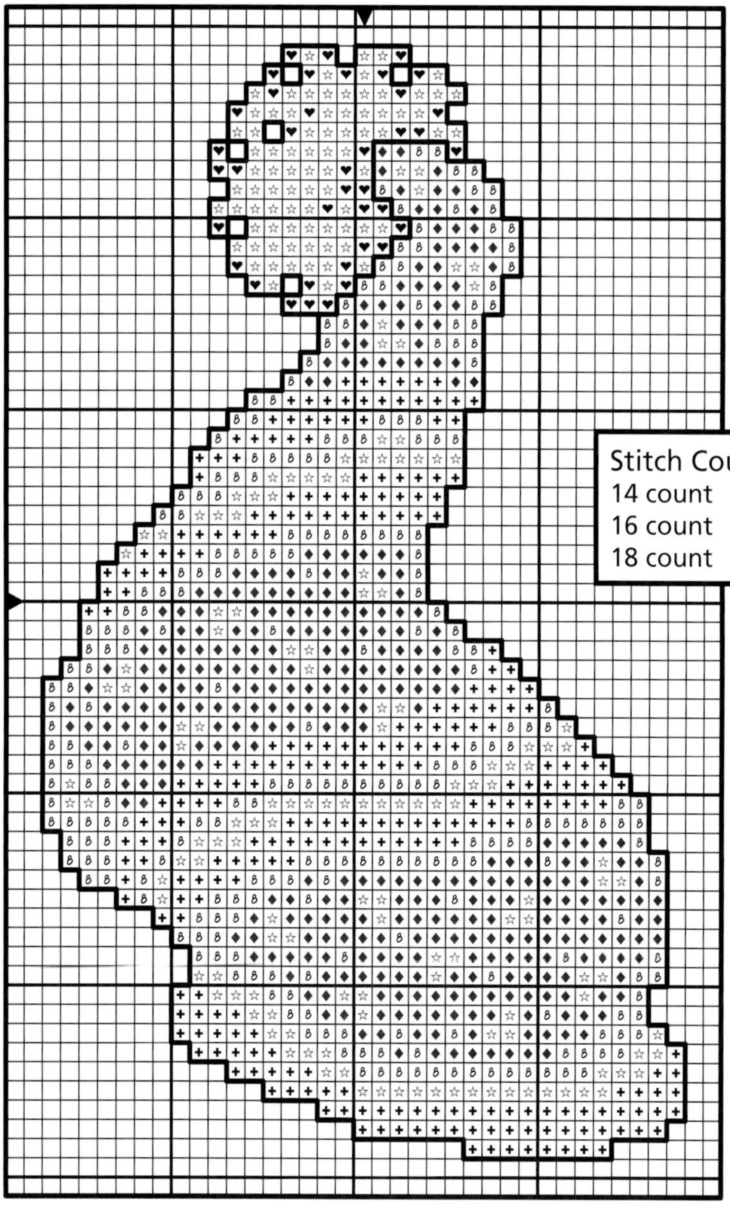

Stitch Count (35w x 58h)	
14 count	2½" x 4¼"
16 count	2¼" x 3⅝"
18 count	2" x 3¼"

BLUE CAP

X	DMC	B'ST	ANC.	COLOR
☆	blanc		2	white
♥	415		398	lt grey
+	703		238	green
8	797	╱	132	dk blue
♦	799		136	lt blue

Design was stitched on a 6½" x 8½" piece of 14 count white Aida (design size 2½" x 4¼"). Three strands of floss were used for Cross Stitch and 1 strand for Backstitch.

Shown on page 3.

ELF WITH LIGHTS

X	DMC	1/4X	B'ST	ANC.	COLOR
☆	blanc			2	white
■	310		╱	403	black
▲	321			9046	red
3	353	3		6	peach
◆◆	553	◆◆		98	dk violet
>	702	>		226	green
◒	726	◒		295	yellow
♥	797	♥		132	dk blue
╱	799			136	lt blue
⬆	995			410	turquoise

Design was stitched on a 7" x 7½" piece of 14 count white Aida (design size 2¾" x 3⅜"). Three strands of floss were used for Cross Stitch and 1 strand for Backstitch.

Shown on page 5.

Stitch Count (38w x 46h)

14 count	2¾" x 3⅜"
16 count	2⅜" x 2⅞"
18 count	2⅛" x 2⅝"

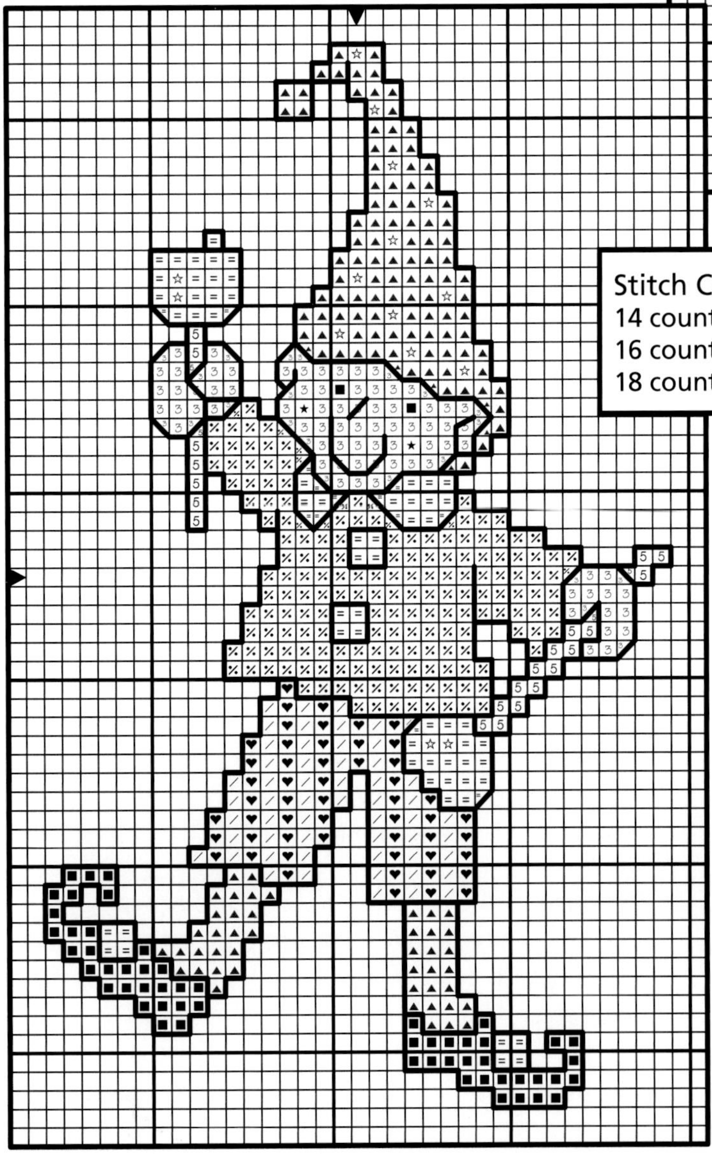

Stitch Count (35w x 57h)

14 count	2½" x 4⅛"
16 count	2¼" x 3⅝"
18 count	2" x 3¼"

BELL-RINGING ELF

X	DMC	1/4X	B'ST	ANC.	COLOR
☆	blanc			2	white
■	310		╱	403	black
▲	321	▲		9046	red
★	352			9	peach
3	353	3		6	lt peach
5	435	5		1046	brown
⁒	701	⁒		227	green
=	726	=		295	yellow
♥	797			132	dk blue
╱	799	╱		136	lt blue

Design was stitched on a 6½" x 8½" piece of 14 count white Aida (design size 2½" x 4⅛"). Three strands of floss were used for Cross Stitch and 1 strand for Backstitch.

Shown on page 5.

Stitch Count (41w x 41h)

14 count	3" x 3"
16 count	2 5/8" x 2 5/8"
18 count	2 3/8" x 2 3/8"

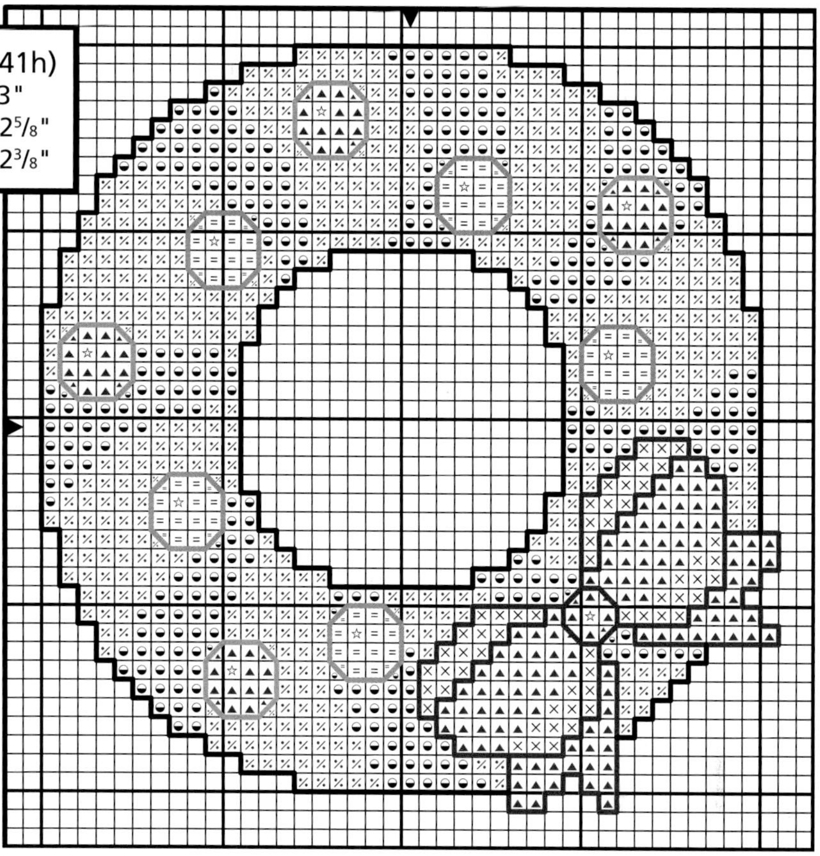

WREATH

X	DMC	1/4X	B'ST	ANC.	COLOR
☆	blanc			2	white
▲	321	◺	/	9046	red
	699		/	923	dk green
⁒	701	◺		227	green
◒	703	◺		238	lt green
=	726	◺	/	295	yellow
	816		/	1005	maroon
☒	3705			35	melon

Design was stitched on a 7" x 7" piece of 14 count white Aida (design size 3" x 3"). Three strands of floss were used for Cross Stitch and 1 strand for Backstitch.

Shown on page 3.

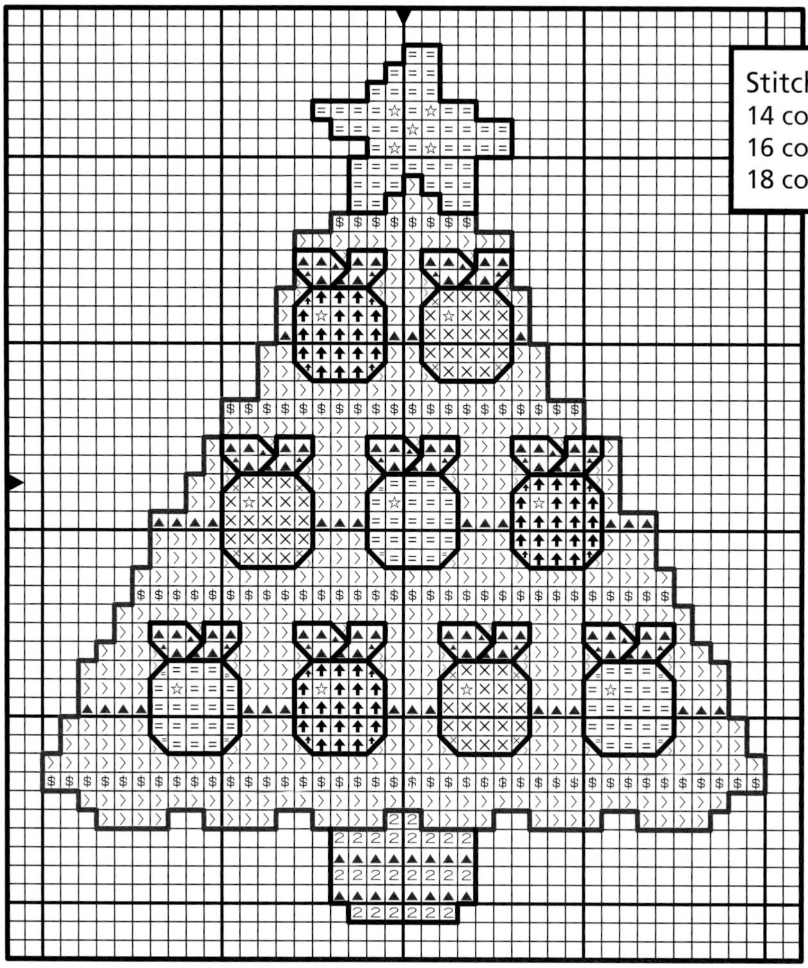

Stitch Count (40w x 47h)

14 count	2 7/8" x 3 3/8"
16 count	2 1/2" x 3"
18 count	2 1/4" x 2 5/8"

TREE

X	DMC	1/4X	B'ST	ANC.	COLOR
☆	blanc			2	white
	310		/	403	black
▲	321	◺		9046	red
$	699		/	923	dk green
>	702	◺		226	green
=	726	◺		295	yellow
2	816			1005	maroon
↑	995	◺		410	turquoise
☒	3705	◺		35	melon

Design was stitched on a 7" x 7 1/2" piece of 14 count white Aida (design size 2 7/8" x 3 3/8"). Three strands of floss were used for Cross Stitch and 1 strand for Backstitch.

Shown on page 3.

POINSETTIA HEART

X	DMC	ANC.	COLOR
▲	321	9046	red
$	699	923	dk green
⁒	702	226	green
=	726	295	yellow
♥	816	1005	maroon
×	3705	35	melon

Design was stitched on a 7½" x 7½" piece of 14 count white Aida (design size 3½" x 3⅜"). Three strands of floss were used for Cross Stitch. Design was also stitched on a 7" x 7" piece of 18 count white Aida (design size 2¾" x 2⅝"). Two strands of floss were used for Cross Stitch. It was inserted in a 3¼" diameter gold-tone frame.

Shown on page 3 and back cover.

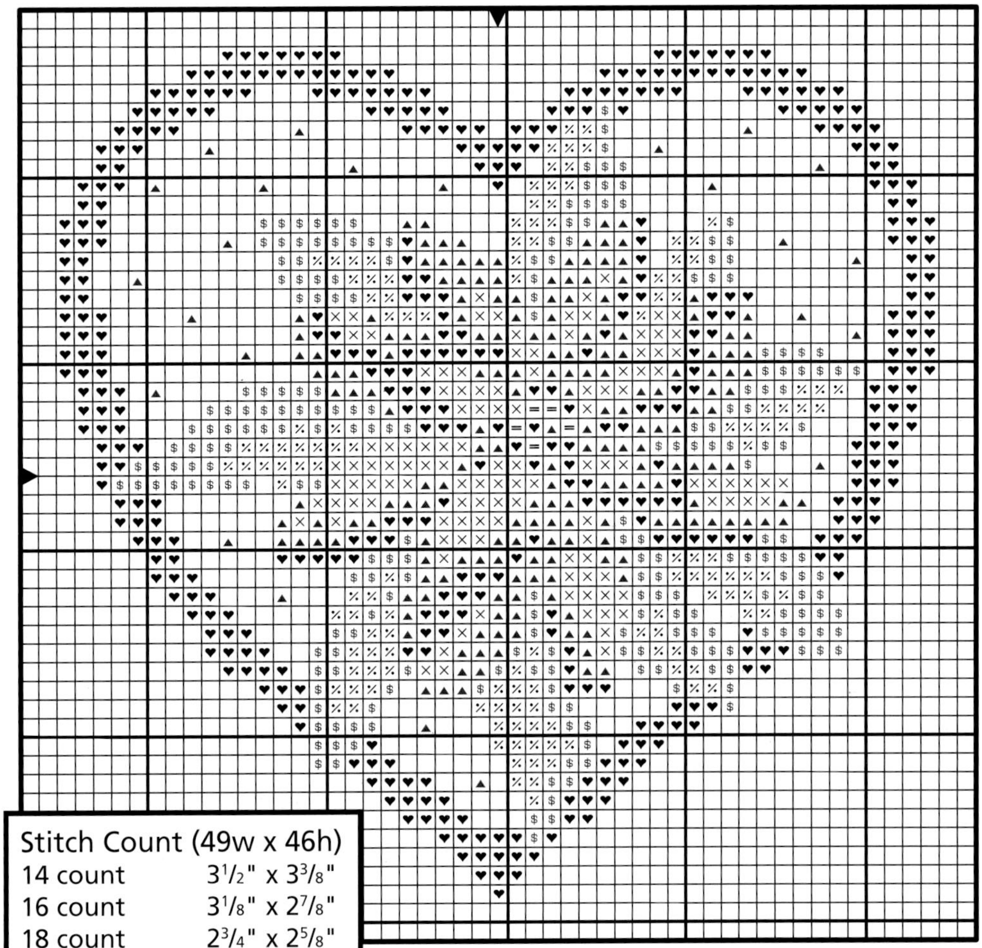

Stitch Count (49w x 46h)

14 count	3½" x 3⅜"
16 count	3⅛" x 2⅞"
18 count	2¾" x 2⅝"

SANTA HAT

X	DMC	B'ST	ANC.	COLOR
☆	blanc		2	white
▲	321		9046	red
$	699	/	923	dk green
⁒	701		227	green
+	703		238	lt green
=	726		295	yellow
◒	762		234	lt grey
♥	816	/	1005	maroon
×	3705		35	melon

Design was stitched on a 7½" x 7½" piece of 14 count white Aida (design size 3⅜" x 3⅛"). Three strands of floss were used for Cross Stitch and 1 strand for Backstitch. Design was also stitched on a 7" x 6½" piece of 18 count white Aida (design size 2⅝" x 2½"). Two strands of floss were used for Cross Stitch and 1 strand for Backstitch. It was inserted in a 3¼" diameter gold-tone frame.

Shown on page 3 and back cover.

Stitch Count (46w x 43h)

14 count	3⅜" x 3⅛"
16 count	2⅞" x 2¾"
18 count	2⅝" x 2½"

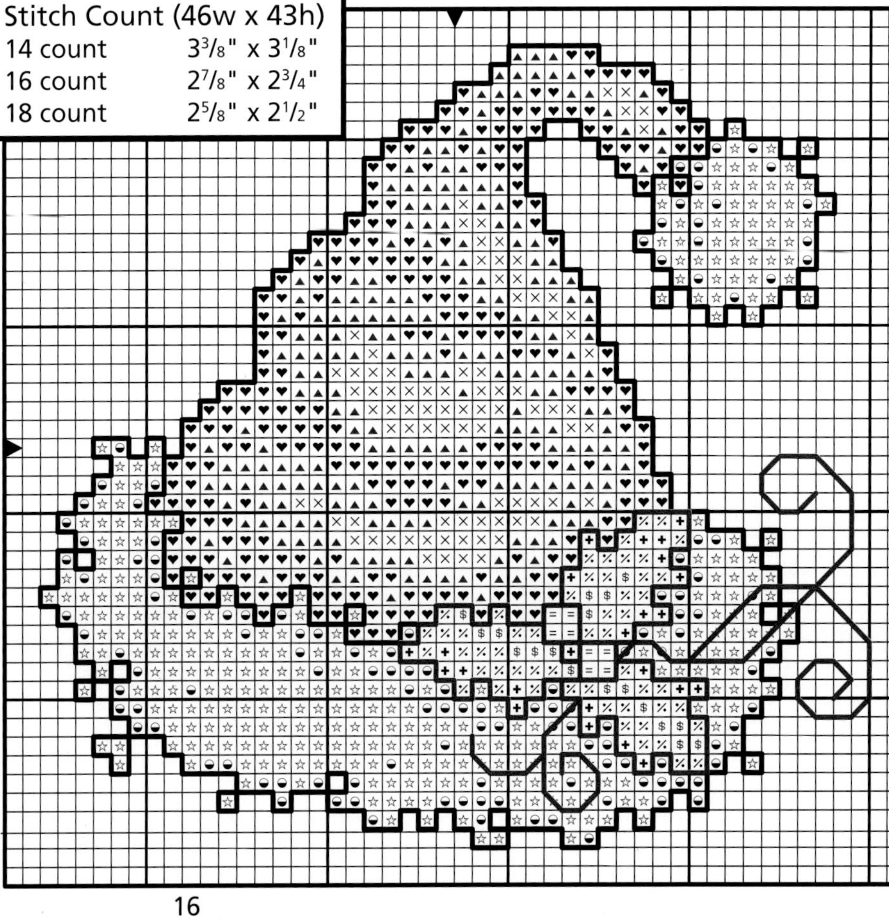

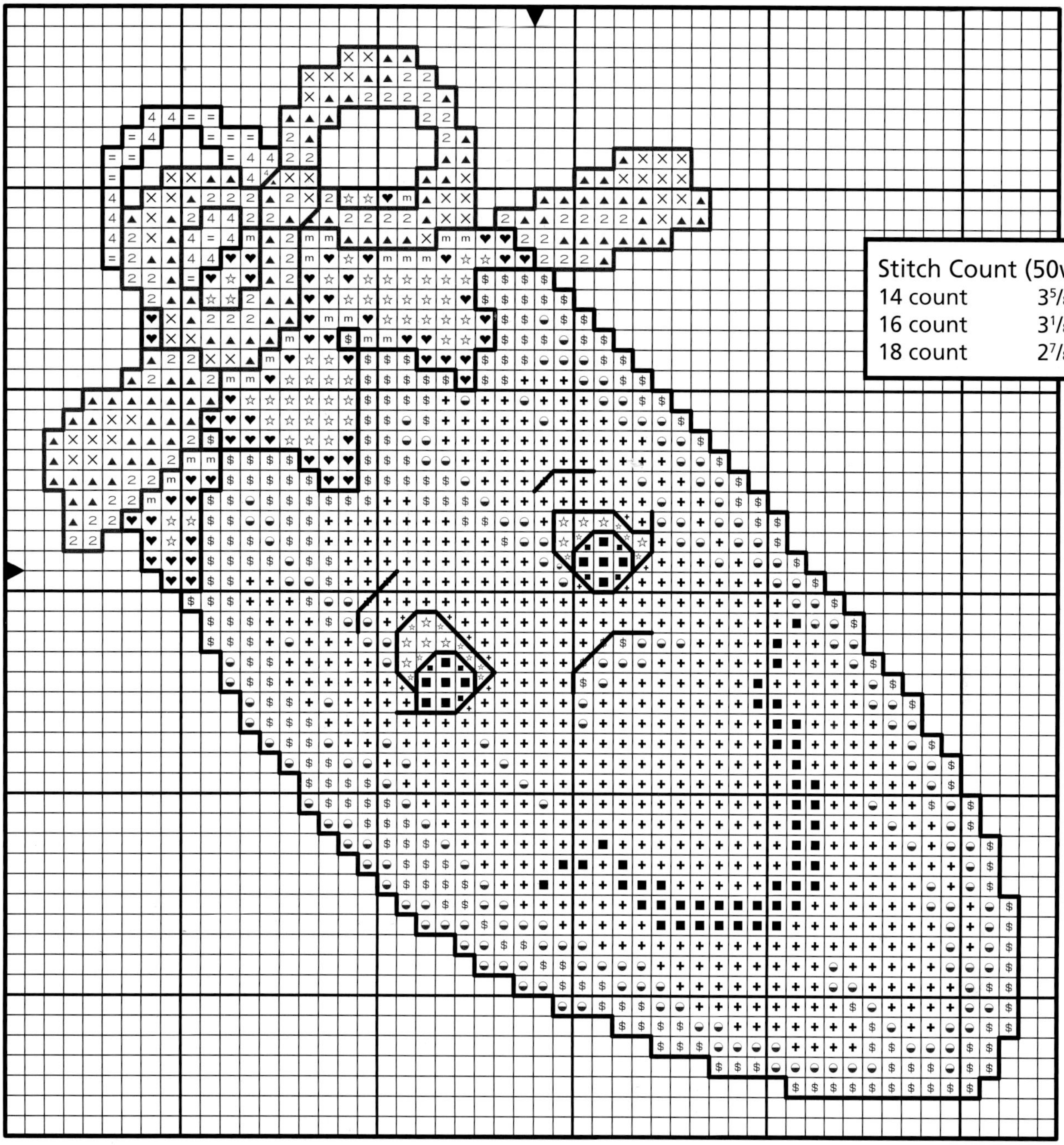

Stitch Count (50w x 52h)	
14 count	3⅝" x 3¾"
16 count	3⅛" x 3¼"
18 count	2⅞" x 3"

GREEN ORNAMENT

X	DMC	¼X	B'ST	ANC.	COLOR
☆	blanc	☆		2	white
■	310	■	/	403	black
m	318			399	grey
▲	321	▲		9046	red
$	699			923	dk green
◒	701	◒		227	green
✚	703	✚		238	lt green
=	726			295	yellow
♥	762			234	lt grey
2	816		/	1005	maroon
✕	3705			35	melon
4	3852	4		306	gold

Design was stitched on an 8" x 8" piece of 14 count white Aida (design size 3⅝" x 3¾"). Three strands of floss were used for Cross Stitch and 1 strand for Backstitch.

Shown on page 3.

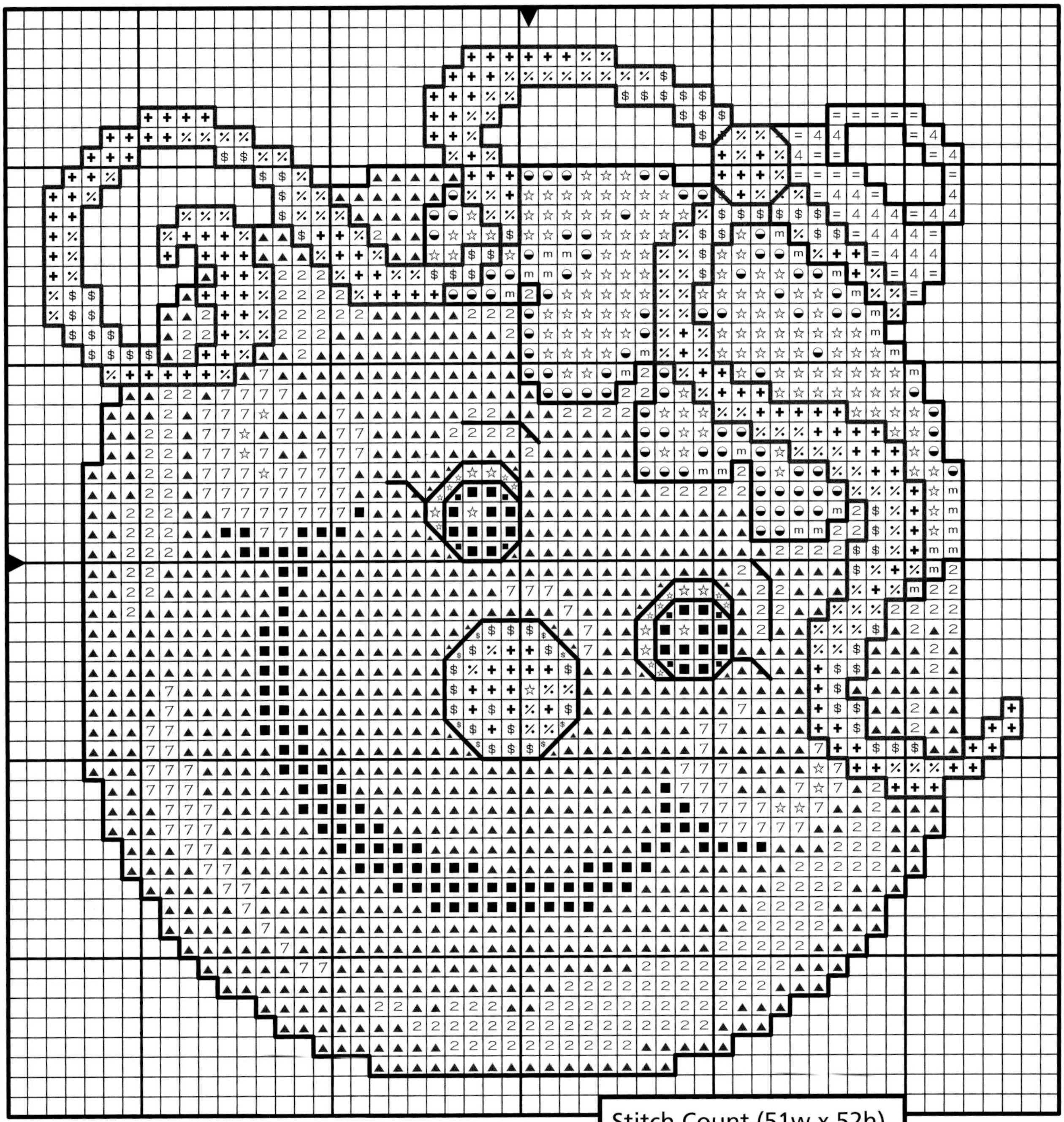

Stitch Count (51w x 52h)	
14 count	3¾" x 3¾"
16 count	3¼" x 3¼"
18 count	2⅞" x 3"

RED ORNAMENT

X	DMC	¼X	B'ST	ANC.	COLOR
☆	blanc	☆		2	white
■	310	■	/	403	black
m	318			399	grey
▲	321	▲		9046	red
$	699	$	/	923	dk green
%	701			227	green
+	703			238	lt green
=	726			295	yellow
◒	762			234	lt grey
2	816			1005	maroon
7	3705			35	lt red
4	3852			306	gold

Design was stitched on an 8" x 8" piece of 14 count white Aida (design size 3¾" x 3¾"). Three strands of floss were used for Cross Stitch and 1 strand for Backstitch.

Shown on page 3.

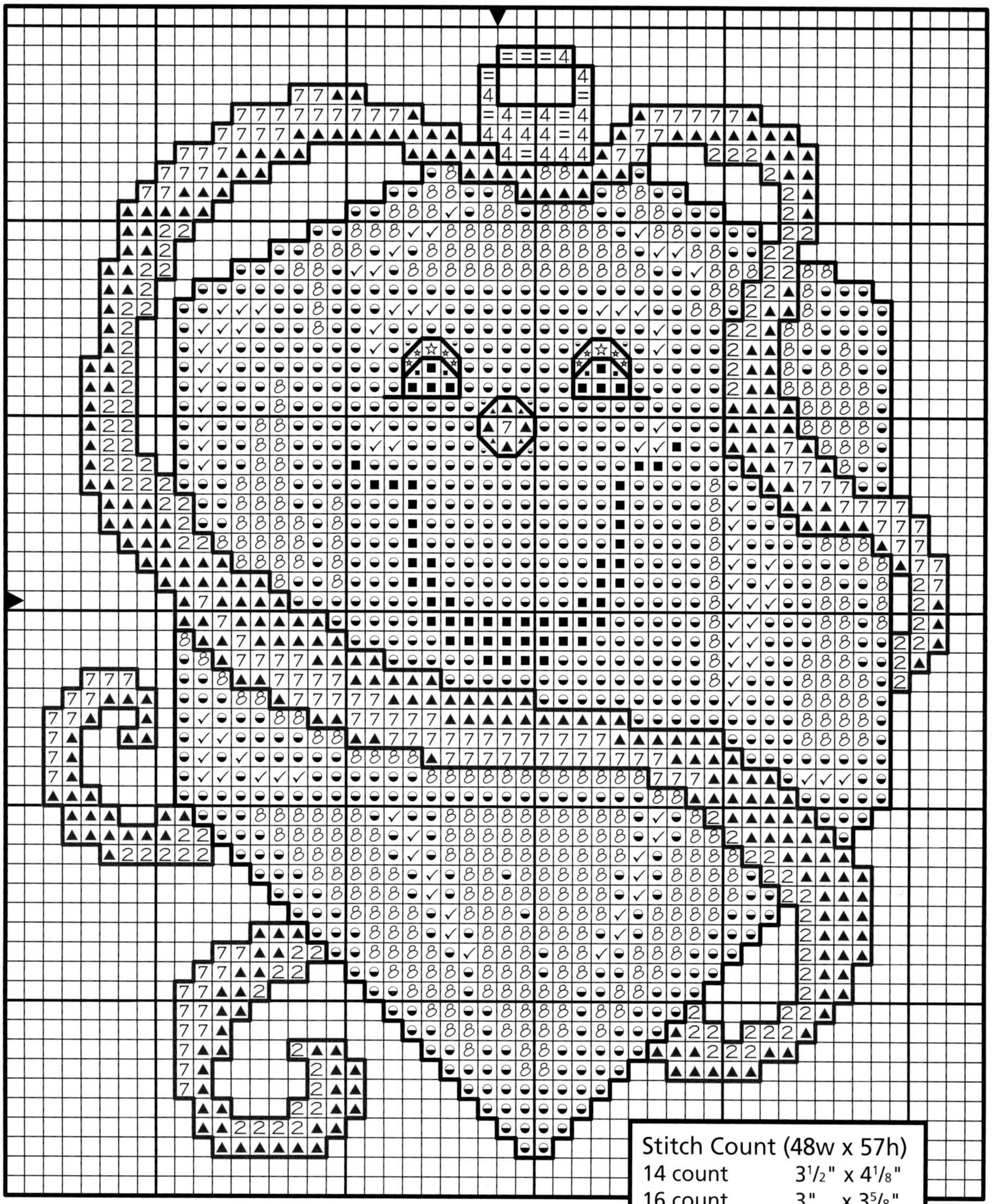

Stitch Count (48w x 57h)	
14 count	$3^1/_2$" x $4^1/_8$"
16 count	3" x $3^5/_8$"
18 count	$2^3/_4$" x $3^1/_4$"

BLUE ORNAMENT

X	DMC	1/4X	B'ST	ANC.	COLOR
☆	blanc	◺☆		2	white
■	310	◺■	/	403	black
▲	321	◺▲		9046	red
=	726			295	lt yellow
8	797			132	dk blue
◒	799	◺◒		136	blue
✓	800			144	lt blue
2	816		/	1005	maroon
7	3705			35	lt red
4	3852			306	gold

Design was stitched on a $7^1/_2$" x $8^1/_2$" piece of 14 count white Aida (design size $3^1/_2$" x $4^1/_8$"). Three strands of floss were used for Cross Stitch and 1 strand for Backstitch.

Shown on page 3.

Stitch Count (52w x 57h)
14 count 3³/₄" x 4¹/₈"
16 count 3¹/₄" x 3⁵/₈"
18 count 3" x 3¹/₄"

REINDEER

X	DMC	¹/₄X	B'ST	ANC.	COLOR
☆	blanc	☆		2	white
■	310	■	/	403	black
▲	321	▲		9046	red
3	351			10	coral
4	433			358	brown
◒	436	◒		1045	tan
◆	554			96	violet
$	699	$	/	923	dk green
+	703			238	green
=	726	=		295	yellow
a	738			361	lt tan
	816		/	1005	maroon
♥	927			848	grey green
↑	995			410	turquoise

Design was stitched on an 8" x 8¹/₂" piece of 14 count white Aida (design size 3³/₄" x 4¹/₈"). Three strands of floss were used for Cross Stitch and 1 strand for Backstitch.

Shown on page 3.

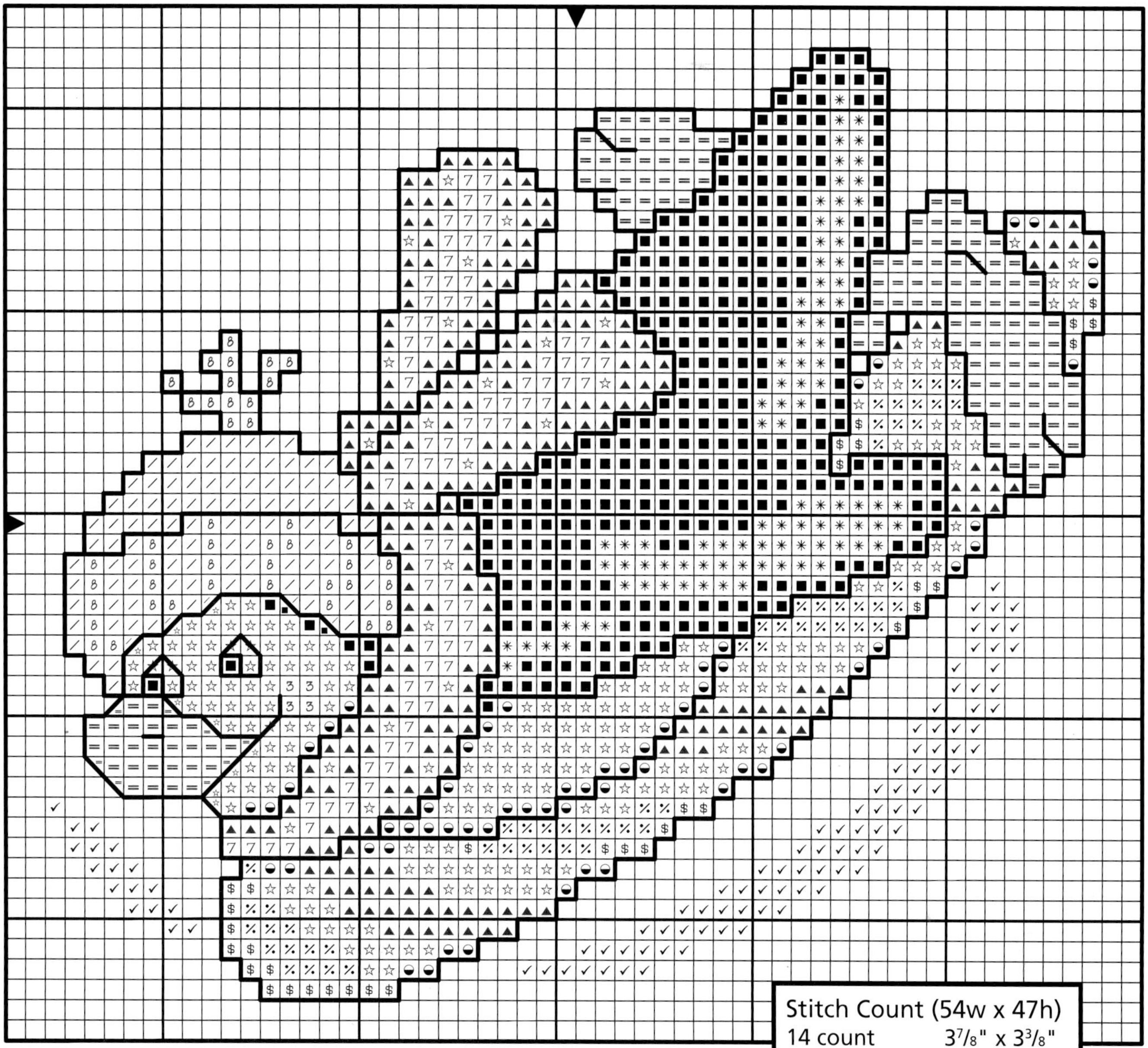

Stitch Count (54w x 47h)	
14 count	$3^{7}/_{8}$" x $3^{3}/_{8}$"
16 count	$3^{3}/_{8}$" x 3"
18 count	3" x $2^{5}/_{8}$"

SLEDDING PENGUIN

X	DMC	1/4X	B'ST	ANC.	COLOR
☆	blanc	☆		2	white
■	310	■	/	403	black
✳	317			400	grey
▲	321			9046	red
3	353			6	peach
◒	415			398	lt grey
$	699			923	dk green
%	701			227	green
=	726	=		295	yellow
8	797			132	dk blue
/	799	/		136	blue
✓	800			144	lt blue
7	3705			35	lt red

Design was stitched on an 8" x $7^{1}/_{2}$" piece of 14 count white Aida (design size $3^{7}/_{8}$" x $3^{3}/_{8}$"). Three strands of floss were used for Cross Stitch and 1 strand for Backstitch.

Shown on page 6.

Stitch Count (55w x 57h)	
14 count	4" x 4 1/8"
16 count	3 1/2" x 3 5/8"
18 count	3 1/8" x 3 1/4"

SKIING PENGUIN

X	DMC	1/4X	B'ST	ANC.	COLOR
☆	blanc	◺☆		2	white
■	310	◺■	/	403	black
m	318			399	grey
▲	321	◺▲		9046	red
◇	415			398	lt grey
◆	554			96	violet

X	DMC	1/4X	ANC.	COLOR
+	703		238	green
=	726	◺=	295	yellow
8	797		132	dk blue
√	800		144	lt blue
2	816	◺2	1005	maroon
×	3705		35	melon

Design was stitched on an 8" x 8 1/2" piece of 14 count white Aida (design size 4" x 4 1/8"). Three strands of floss were used for Cross Stitch and 1 strand for Backstitch.

Shown on page 6.

Stitch Count (44w x 58h)	
14 count	$3^1/_8$" x $4^1/_4$"
16 count	$2^3/_4$" x $3^5/_8$"
18 count	$2^1/_2$" x $3^1/_4$"

PENGUIN WITH CANDY CANE

X	DMC	¼X	B'ST	ANC.	COLOR
☆	blanc	☆		2	white
■	310		/	403	black
✳	317			400	grey
▲	321			9046	red
◇	415			398	lt grey
$	699	$		923	dk green

X	DMC	¼X	ANC.	COLOR
◒	702		226	green
=	726	=	295	yellow
2	816		1005	maroon
X	3705		35	melon

Design was stitched on a $7^1/_2$" x $8^1/_2$" piece of 14 count white Aida (design size $3^1/_8$" x $4^1/_4$"). Three strands of floss were used for Cross Stitch and 1 strand for Backstitch.

Shown on page 6.

Stitch Count (52w x 56h)

14 count	3³/₄" x 4"
16 count	3¹/₄" x 3¹/₂"
18 count	3" x 3¹/₈"

REDBIRD

X	DMC	¹/₄X	B'ST	ANC.	COLOR
☆	blanc			2	white
■	310	■	/	403	black
▲	321	▲		9046	red
♥	350	♥		11	coral
★	352			9	peach
$	699			923	dk green
=	726	=		295	yellow
◒	783	◒		306	gold
2	816	2		1005	maroon

Design was stitched on an 8" x 8" piece of 14 count white Aida (design size 3³/₄" x 4"). Three strands of floss were used for Cross Stitch and 1 strand for Backstitch. Design was also stitched on a 7" x 7¹/₂" piece of 18 count white Aida (design size 3" x 3¹/₈"). Two strands of floss were used for Cross Stitch and 1 strand for Backstitch. It was inserted in a 3¹/₄" diameter gold-tone frame.

Shown on page 6 and back cover.

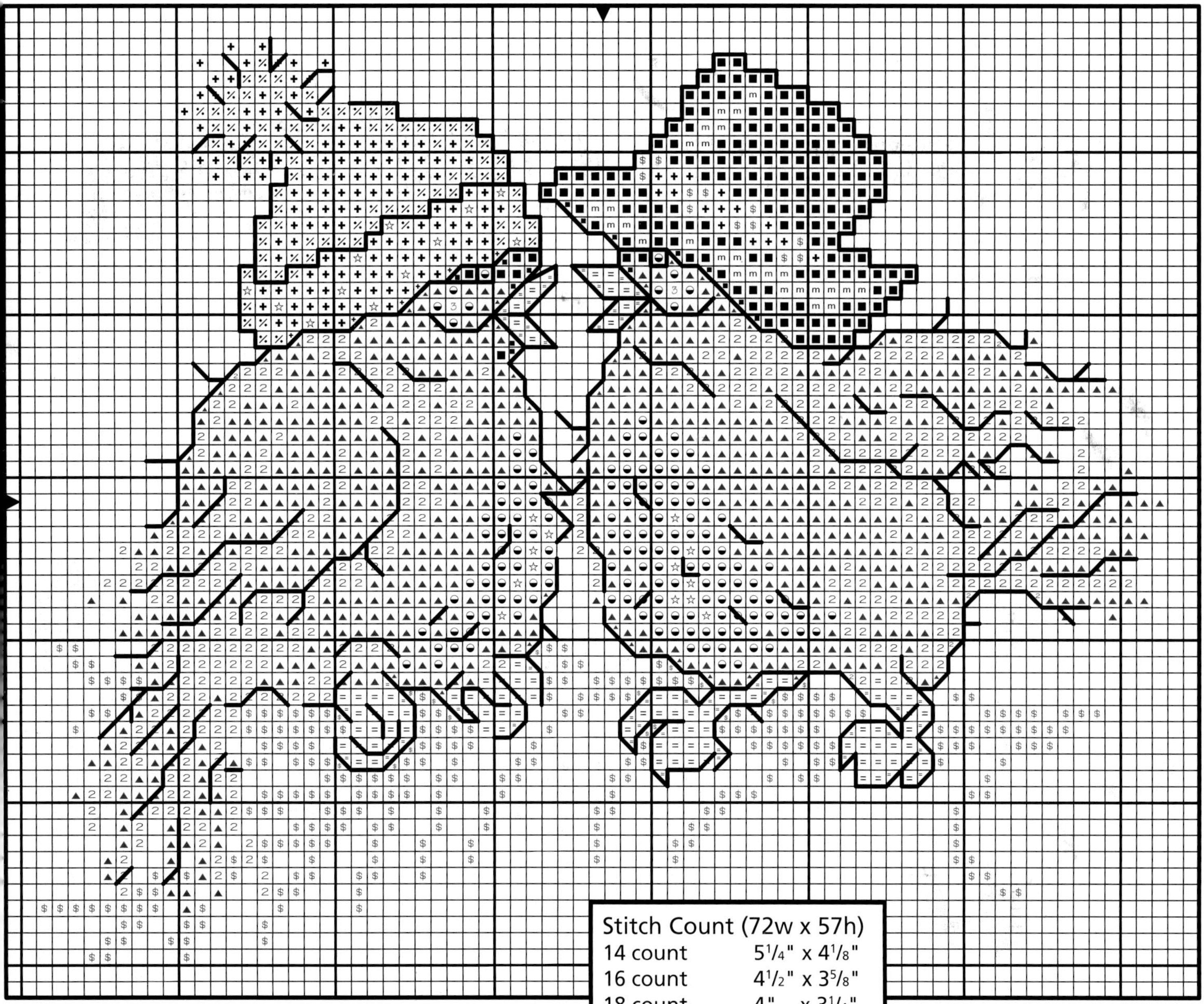

Stitch Count (72w x 57h)

14 count	$5^1/_4$" x $4^1/_8$"
16 count	$4^1/_2$" x $3^5/_8$"
18 count	4" x $3^1/_4$"

REDBIRD COUPLE

X	DMC	¼X	B'ST	ANC.	COLOR
☆	blanc			2	white
■	310	◪	/	403	black
m	318			399	grey
▲	321	◪		9046	red
◒	352			9	peach
3	353			6	lt peach
$	699	◪		923	dk green
%	701			227	green
+	703	◪		238	lt green
=	726	◪		295	yellow
2	816	◪		1005	maroon

Design was stitched on a $9^1/_2$" x $8^1/_2$" piece of 14 count white Aida (design size $5^1/_4$" x $4^1/_8$"). Three strands of floss were used for Cross Stitch and 1 strand for Backstitch.

Shown on page 6.

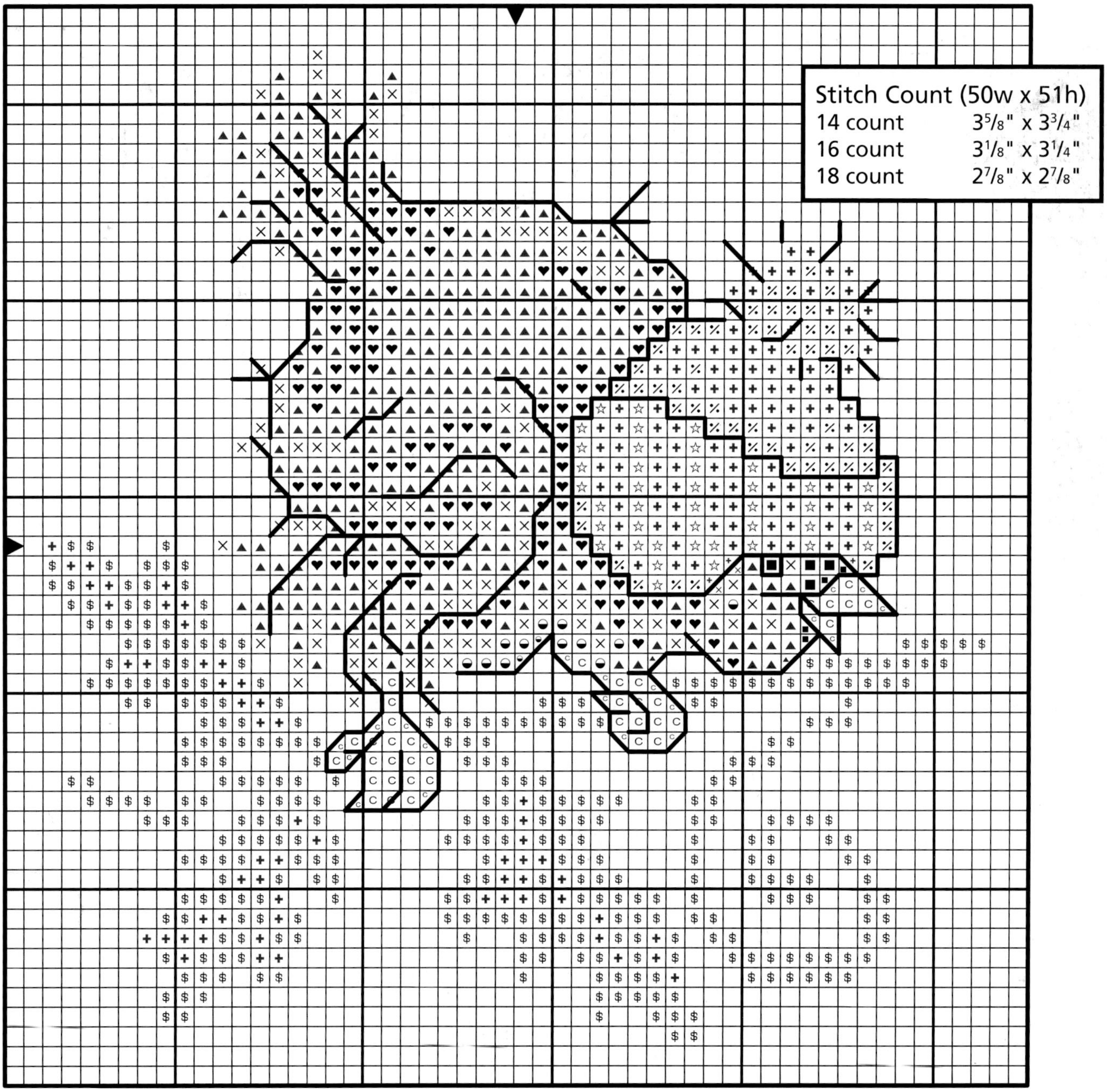

REDBIRD WITH GREEN CAP

X	DMC	1/4X	B'ST	ANC.	COLOR
☆	blanc			2	white
■	310	◪	╱	403	black
▲	321	◪		9046	red
◒	351	◪		10	coral
✕	353	◪		6	peach
$	699			923	dk green
⁒	701			227	green
+	703	◪		238	lt green
c	726	◪		295	yellow
♥	816			1005	maroon

Design was stitched on an 8" x 8" piece of 14 count white Aida (design size 3 5/8" x 3 3/4"). Three strands of floss were used for Cross Stitch and 1 strand for Backstitch. Design was also stitched on a 7" x 7" piece of 18 count white Aida (design size 2 7/8" x 2 7/8"). Two strands of floss were used for Cross Stitch and 1 strand for Backstitch. It was inserted in a 3 1/4" diameter gold-tone frame.

Shown on page 6 and back cover.

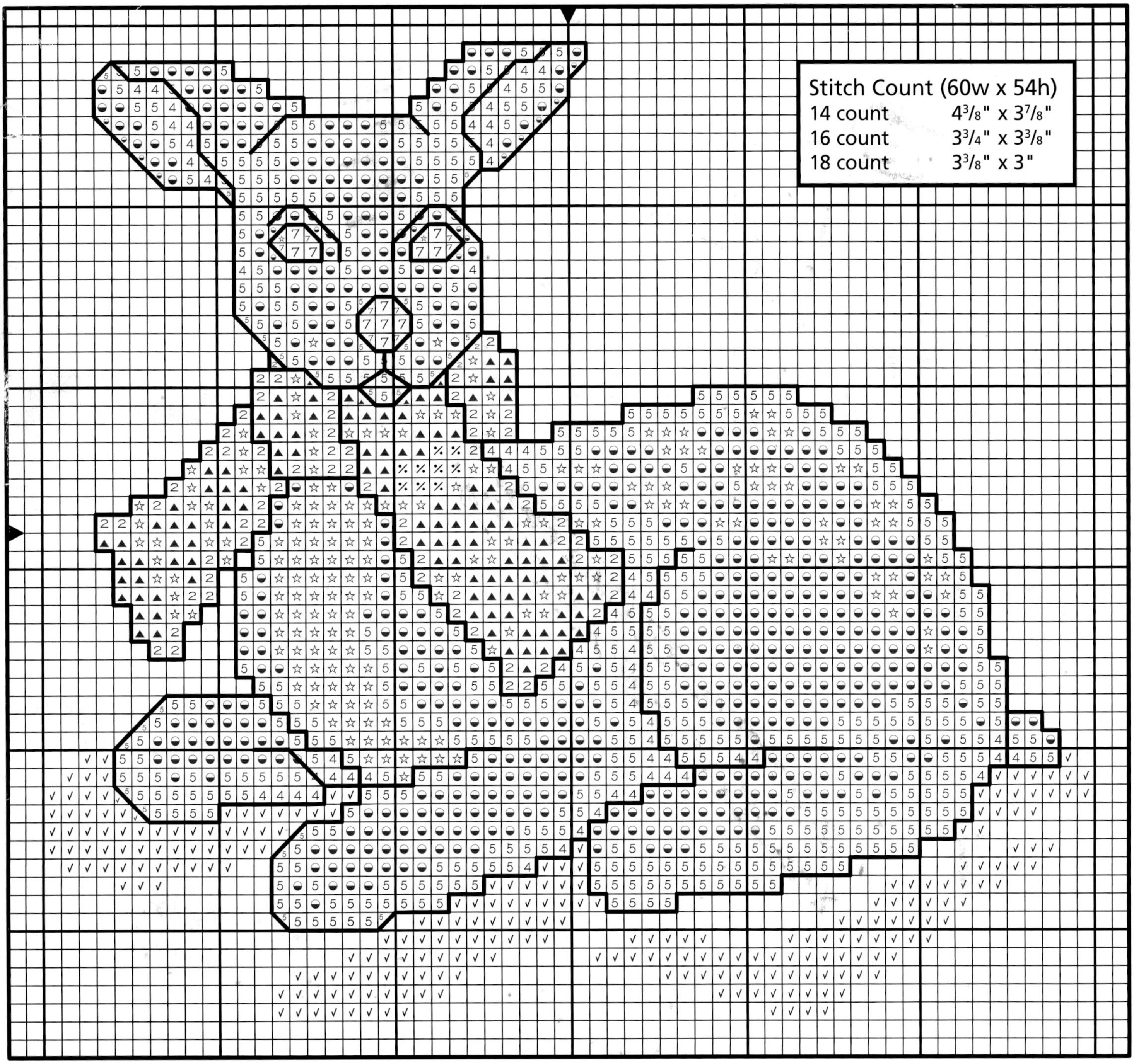

Stitch Count (60w x 54h)	
14 count	4³/₈" x 3⁷/₈"
16 count	3³/₄" x 3³/₈"
18 count	3³/₈" x 3"

BAISBY DEER

X	DMC	¹/₄X	B'ST	ANC.	COLOR
☆	blanc	☆		2	white
▲	321	▲		9046	red
4	433			358	dk brown
5	435	5		1046	brown
◒	437	◒		362	dk tan
⁒	701			227	green
√	800	√		144	lt blue
2	816	2		1005	maroon
7	3371	7	/	382	black brown

Design was stitched on an 8¹/₂" x 8" piece of 14 count white Aida (design size 4³/₈" x 3⁷/₈"). Three strands of floss were used for Cross Stitch and 1 strand for Backstitch.

Shown on page 6.

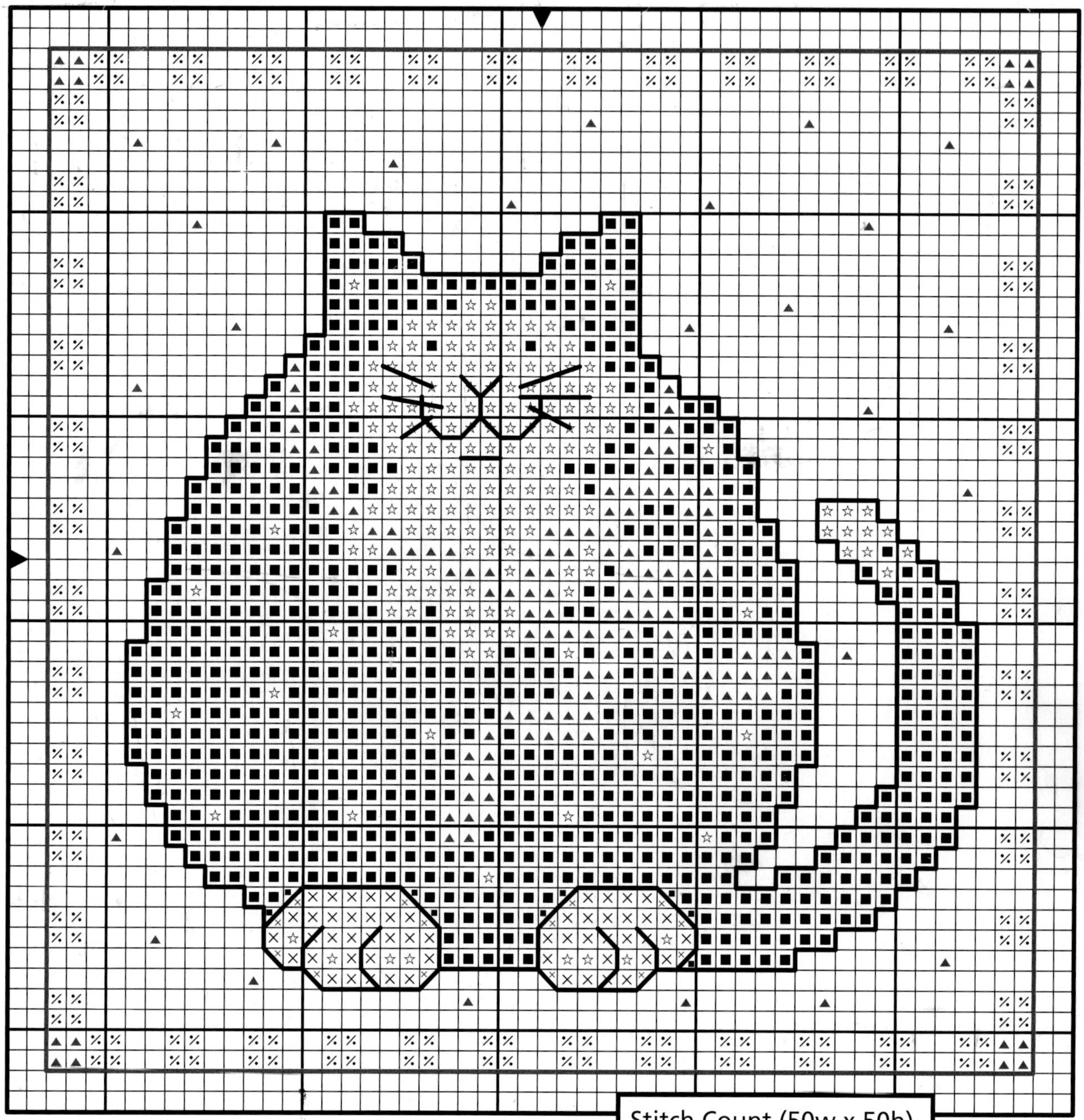

Stitch Count (50w x 50h)	
14 count	$3^5/_8$" x $3^5/_8$"
16 count	$3^1/_8$" x $3^1/_8$"
18 count	$2^7/_8$" x $2^7/_8$"

CAT

X	DMC	¼X	B'ST	ANC.	COLOR
☆	blanc			2	white
■	310	◪	/	403	black
▲	321			9046	red
⁒	701			227	green
☒	762	⧄		234	lt grey
	3821		/	305	gold

Design was stitched on an 8" x 8" piece of 14 count white Aida (design size $3^5/_8$" x $3^5/_8$"). Three strands of floss were used for Cross Stitch and 1 strand for Backstitch.

Shown on page 6.

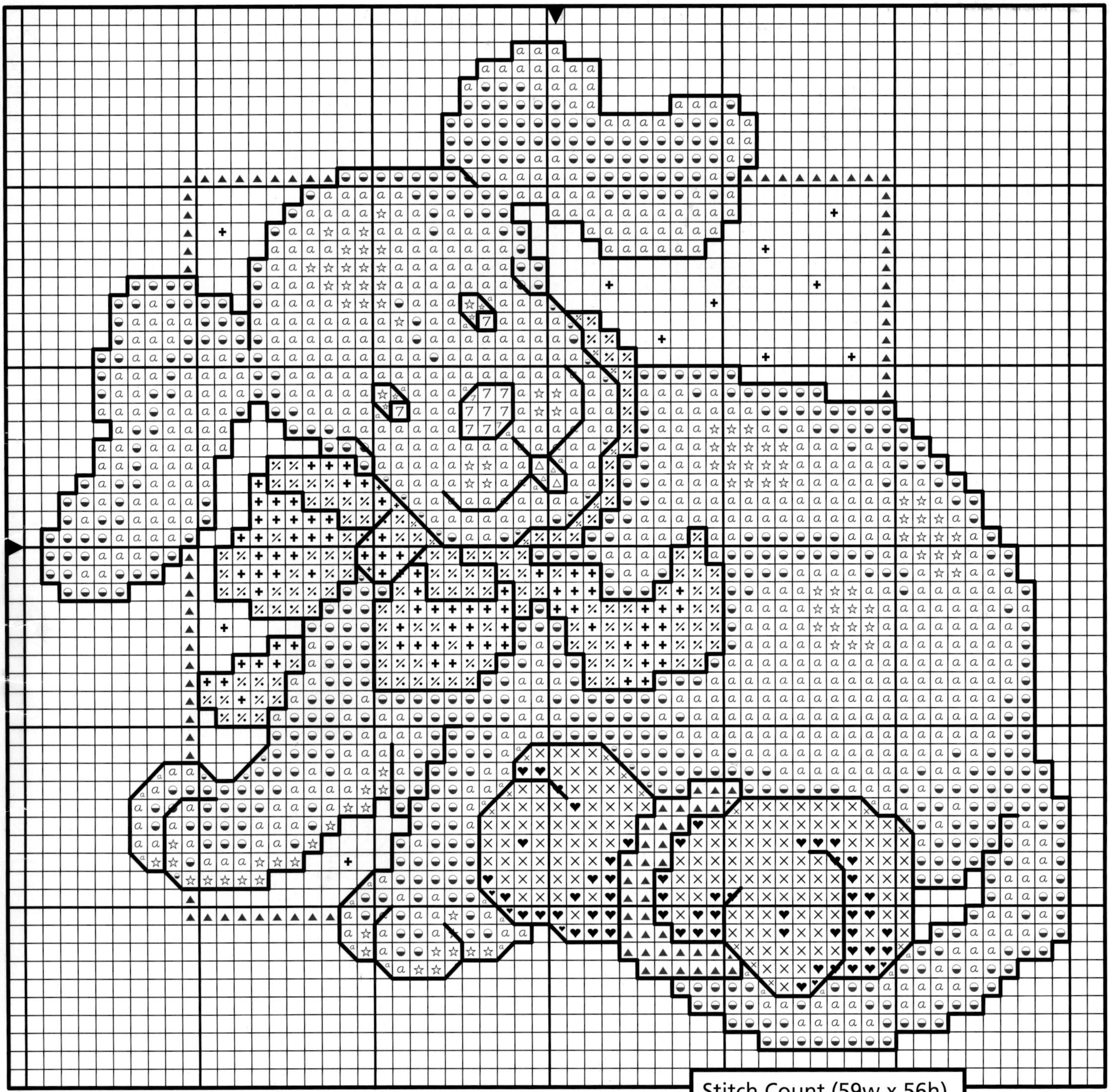

Stitch Count (55w x 52h)	
14 count	4" x $3^3/_4$"
16 count	$3^1/_2$" x $3^1/_4$"
18 count	$3^1/_8$" x 3"

PEACE BEARS

X	DMC	1/4X	B'ST	ANC.	COLOR
☆	blanc	☆		2	white
■	310	■	/	403	black
◆	318	◆		399	grey
$	699		/	923	dk green
+	703			238	green
↑	762	↑		234	lt grey

Design was stitched on an 8" x 8" piece of 14 count white Aida (design size 4" x $3^3/_4$"). Three strands of floss were used for Cross Stitch and 1 strand for Backstitch.

Shown on page 6.

Stitch Count (58w x 53h)

14 count	4¼" x 3⅞"
16 count	3⅝" x 3⅜"
18 count	3¼" x 3"

GINGERBREAD COUPLE

X	DMC	¼X	B'ST	ANC.	COLOR
☆	blanc	☆		2	white
■	310	■	/	403	black
▲	321	▲	/	9046	red
◆	415	◆		398	lt grey
5	435	5		1046	brown
⁒	701	⁒		227	green
+	703			238	lt green
=	726			295	yellow
a	738	a		361	lt tan
/	799	/		136	lt blue
H	801	H		359	dk brown
2	816	2		1005	maroon
✕	3705			35	melon

Design was stitched on an 8½" x 8" piece of 14 count white Aida (design size 4¼" x 3⅞"). Three strands of floss were used for Cross Stitch and 1 strand for Backstitch.

Shown on page 5.

Stitch Count (53w x 58h)	
14 count	$3^{7}/_{8}$" x $4^{1}/_{4}$"
16 count	$3^{3}/_{8}$" x $3^{5}/_{8}$"
18 count	3" x $3^{1}/_{4}$"

GINGERBREAD DRUMMER MITTEN

X	DMC	1/4X	B'ST	ANC.	COLOR
☆	blanc	☆		2	white
■	310		/	403	black
▲	321	▲	/	9046	red
5	435	5		1046	brown
◒	437	◒		362	tan
$	699	$		923	dk green
>	702			226	green
♥	726	♥		295	yellow
H	801			359	dk brown
X	3705			35	melon

Design was stitched on an 8" x $8^{1}/_{2}$" piece of 14 count white Aida (design size $3^{7}/_{8}$" x $4^{1}/_{4}$"). Three strands of floss were used for Cross Stitch and 1 strand for Backstitch.

Shown on page 5.

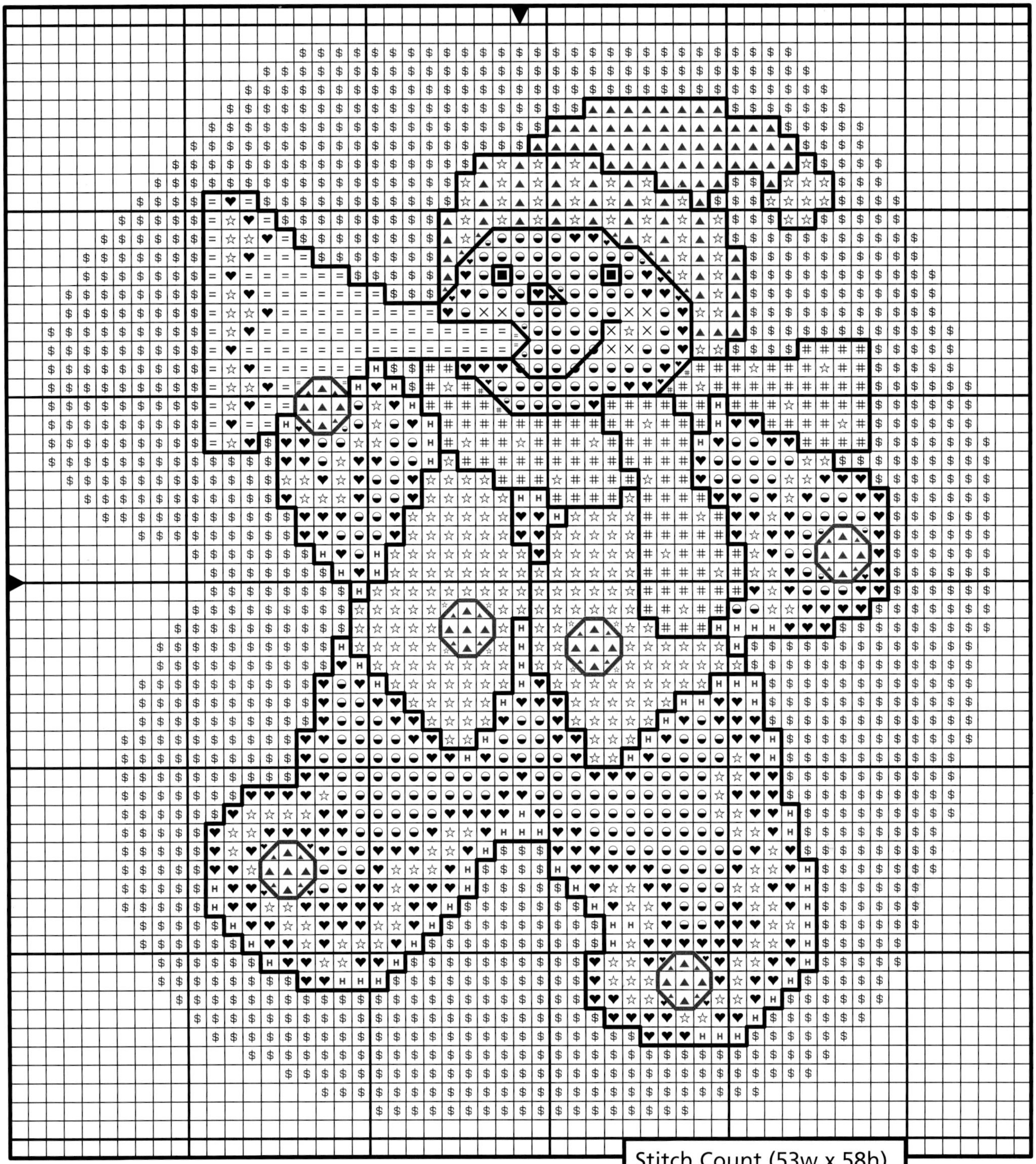

Stitch Count (53w x 58h)	
14 count	3 7/8" x 4 1/4"
16 count	3 3/8" x 3 5/8"
18 count	3" x 3 1/4"

GINGERBREAD BUGLER MITTEN

X	DMC	1/4X	B'ST	ANC.	COLOR
☆	blanc			2	white
■	310		/	403	black
▲	321	◺▲	/	9046	red
♥	435	◺♥		1046	brown
◒	437	◺◒		362	tan
$	699			923	dk green
=	726	◺=		295	yellow
H	801			359	dk brown
#	996	◺#		433	turquoise
✕	3705			35	melon

Design was stitched on an 8" x 8 1/2" piece of 14 count white Aida (design size 3 7/8" x 4 1/4"). Three strands of floss were used for Cross Stitch and 1 strand for Backstitch.

Shown on page 5.

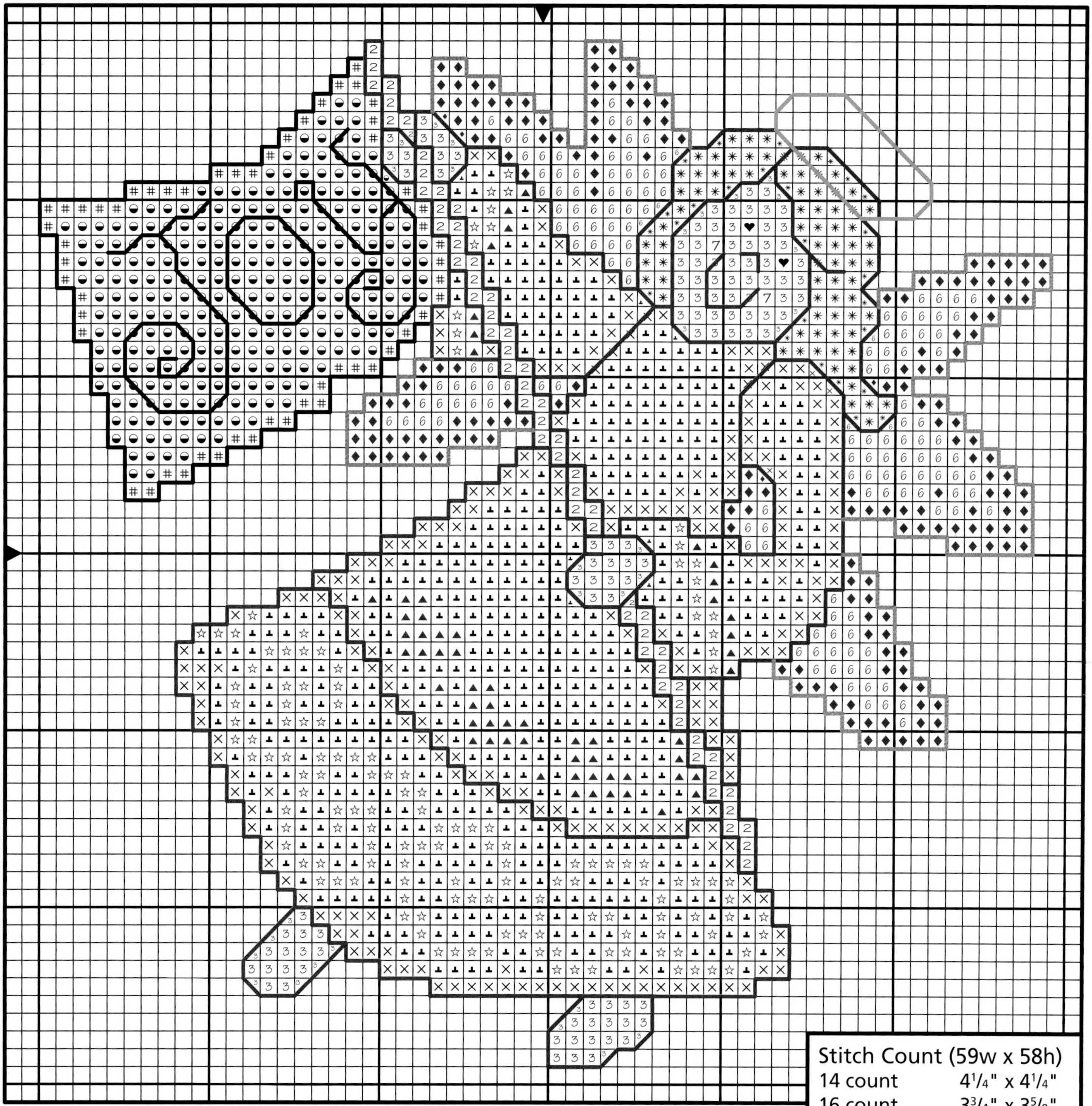

Stitch Count (59w x 58h)

14 count	$4^1/_4$" x $4^1/_4$"
16 count	$3^3/_4$" x $3^5/_8$"
18 count	$3^3/_8$" x $3^1/_4$"

JOY ANGEL

X	DMC	1/4X	B'ST	ANC.	COLOR
☆	blanc			2	white
♥	300		/	352	brown
▲	321			9046	red
3	353	3		6	peach
♦	676	♦		891	gold
	726		/*	295	yellow
6	746	6		275	cream
	797		/	132	dk blue
◒	800	◒		144	lt blue
#	809			130	blue
2	816	2	/	1005	maroon
⊥	963	⊥		73	lt rose
✳	976	✳		1001	golden brown
7	3705			35	melon
⊠	3716	⊠		25	rose

*Use 2 strands.

Design was stitched on an $8^1/_2$" x $8^1/_2$" piece of 14 count white Aida (design size $4^1/_4$" x $4^1/_4$"). Three strands of floss were used for Cross Stitch and 1 strand for Backstitch unless otherwise noted.

Shown on page 6.

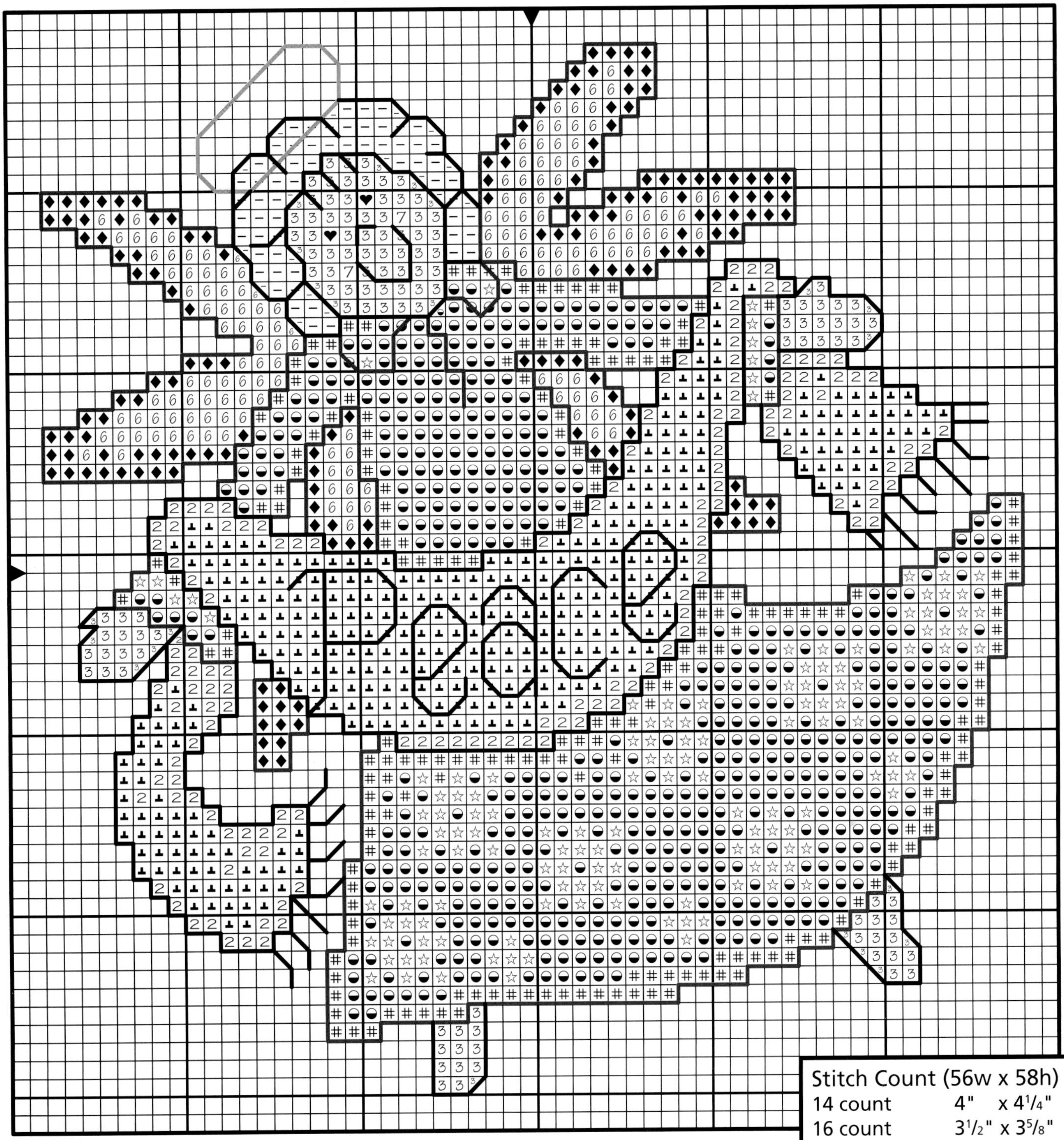

Stitch Count (56w x 58h)

14 count	4" x 4 1/4"
16 count	3 1/2" x 3 5/8"
18 count	3 1/8" x 3 1/4"

PEACE ANGEL

X	DMC	1/4X	B'ST	ANC.	COLOR
☆	blanc			2	white
♥	300		/	352	brown
3	353	3		6	peach
♦	676			891	gold
	726		/*	295	yellow
6	746	6		275	cream
	797		/	132	dk blue

X	DMC	1/4X	ANC.	COLOR
◒	800	◒	144	lt blue
#	809		130	blue
⊥	963		73	lt rose
−	970	−	316	orange
7	3705		35	melon
2	3716	2	25	rose

*Use 2 strands.

Design was stitched on an 8" x 8 1/2" piece of 14 count white Aida (design size 4" x 4 1/4"). Three strands of floss were used for Cross Stitch and 1 strand for Backstitch unless otherwise noted.

Shown on page 6.

Stitch Count (56w x 59h)

14 count	4"	x $4^1/_4$"
16 count	$3^1/_2$"	x $3^3/_4$"
18 count	$3^1/_8$"	x $3^3/_8$"

CAROLING BOY

X	DMC	$^1/_4$X	ANC.	COLOR
☆	blanc	☆	2	white
m	318	m	399	grey
▲	321	▲	9046	red
◒	352	◒	9	peach
3	353	3	6	lt peach
✖	415		398	lt grey
△	436	△	1045	tan
⁒	701	⁒	227	green

X	DMC	$^1/_4$X	B'ST	ANC.	COLOR
+	703	+		238	lt green
=	726	=		295	yellow
8	797	8	/	132	dk blue
♥	798	♥		131	blue
/	799	/		136	lt blue
2	816	2		1005	maroon
■	3371	■	/	382	black brown

Design was stitched on an 8" x $8^1/_2$" piece of 14 count white Aida (design size 4" x $4^1/_4$"). Three strands of floss were used for Cross Stitch and 1 strand for Backstitch.

Shown on page 5.

Stitch Count (56w x 59h)	
14 count	4" x 4 1/4"
16 count	3 1/2" x 3 3/4"
18 count	3 1/8" x 3 3/8"

CAROLING GIRL

X	DMC	1/4X	ANC.	COLOR
☆	blanc	◿☆	2	white
✱	317		400	dk grey
m	318		399	grey
▲	321	◿▲	9046	red
◒	352	◿◒	9	peach
3	353	◿3	6	lt peach
✖	415	◿✖	398	lt grey

X	DMC	1/4X	B'ST	ANC.	COLOR
△	436	◿△		1045	tan
⁒	701	◿⁒		227	green
+	703	◿+		238	lt green
	797		/	132	dk blue
/	799	◿		136	lt blue
2	816			1005	maroon
■	3371	◿■	/	382	black brown

Design was stitched on an 8" x 8 1/2" piece of 14 count white Aida (design size 4" x 4 1/4"). Three strands of floss were used for Cross Stitch.

Shown on page 5.

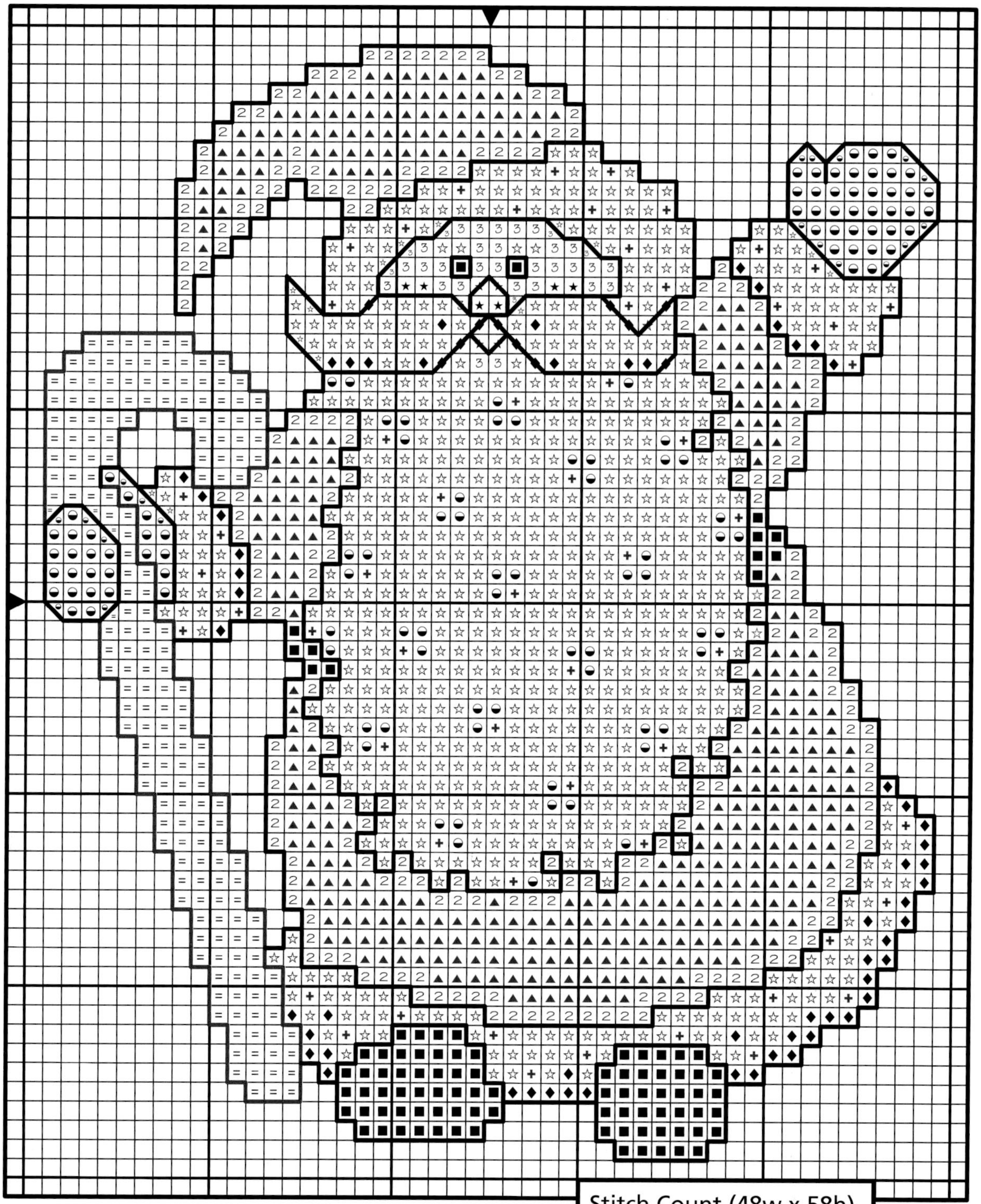

Stitch Count (48w x 58h)	
14 count	3½" x 4¼"
16 count	3" x 3⅝"
18 count	2¾" x 3¼"

HAPPY SANTA

X	DMC	¼X	B'ST	ANC.	COLOR
☆	blanc	☆		2	white
■	310		/	403	black
▲	321			9046	red
★	352			9	peach
3	353	3		6	lt peach
◆	415			398	lt grey
◒	701	◒		227	green
+	703			238	lt green
=	726	=		295	yellow
2	816		/	1005	maroon

Design was stitched on a 7½" x 8½" piece of 14 count white Aida (design size 3½" x 4¼"). Three strands of floss were used for Cross Stitch and 1 strand for Backstitch.

Shown on page 5.

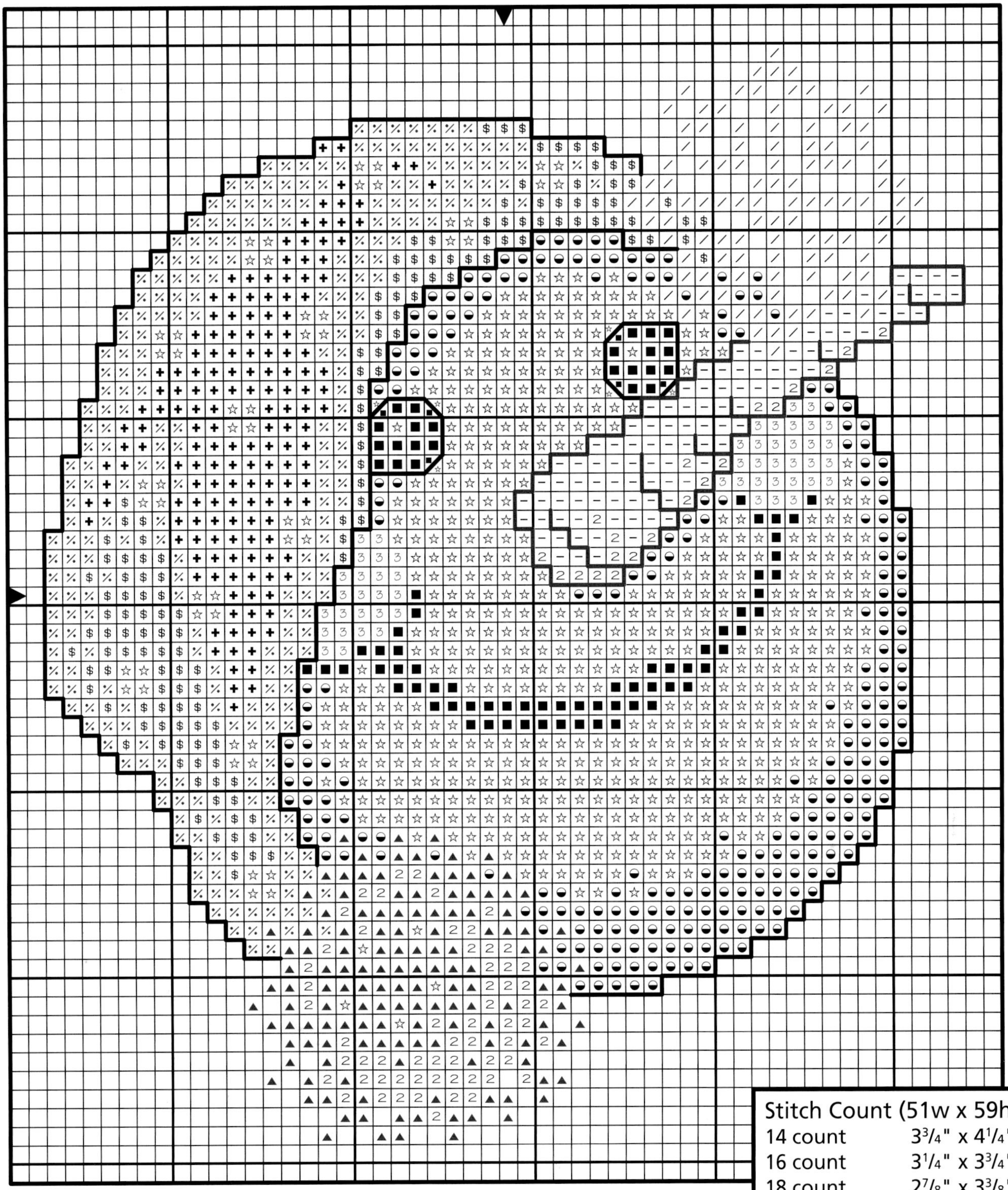

Stitch Count (51w x 59h)

14 count	$3^3/_4$" x $4^1/_4$"
16 count	$3^1/_4$" x $3^3/_4$"
18 count	$2^7/_8$" x $3^3/_8$"

SNOWMAN HEAD

X	DMC	1/4X	B'ST	ANC.	COLOR
☆	blanc	☆		2	white
■	310	■	/	403	black
▲	321			9046	red
3	353			6	peach
$	699			923	dk green
⁒	701			227	green

X	DMC	B'ST	ANC.	COLOR
+	703		238	lt green
◒	762		234	lt grey
/	799		136	blue
2	816	/	1005	maroon
−	970		316	orange

Design was stitched on an 8" x $8^1/_2$" piece of 14 count white Aida (design size $3^3/_4$" x $4^1/_4$"). Three strands of floss were used for Cross Stitch and 1 strand for Backstitch.

Shown on page 4.

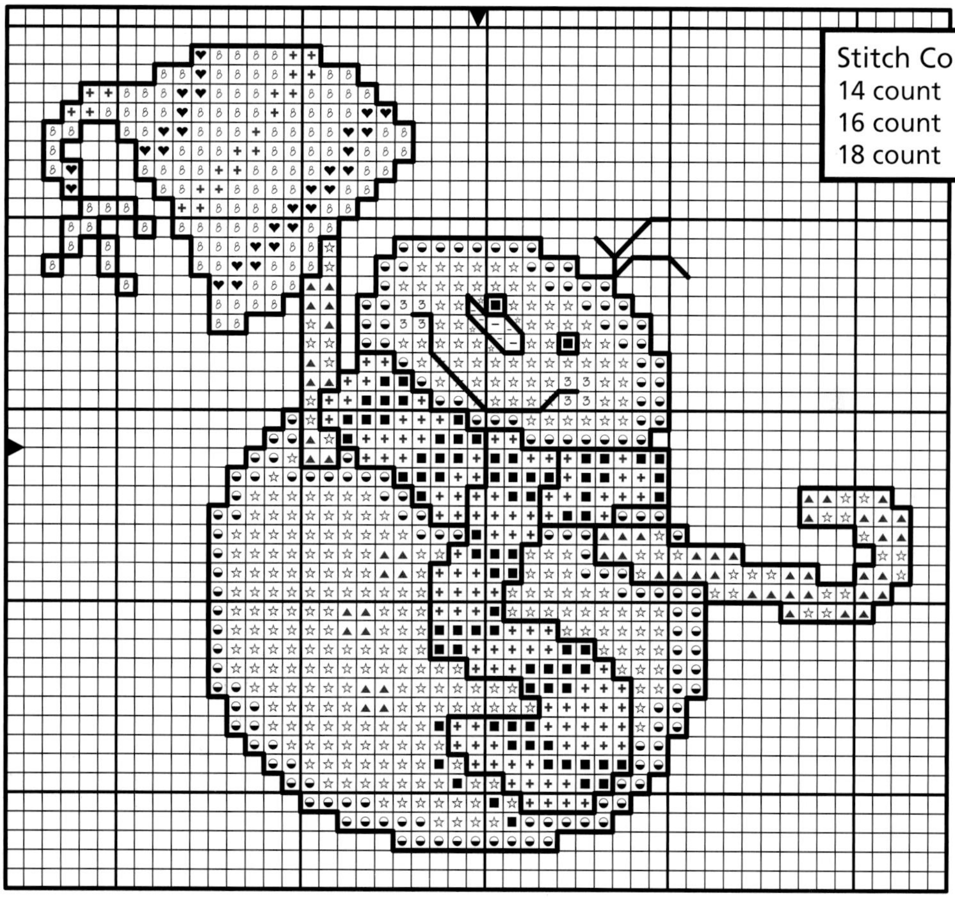

Stitch Count (47w x 42h)
14 count 3 3/8" x 3"
16 count 3" x 2 5/8"
18 count 2 5/8" x 2 3/8"

SNOWBABY WITH BLUE CAP

X	DMC	1/4X	B'ST	ANC.	COLOR
☆	blanc	☆		2	white
■	310		/	403	black
▲	321			9046	red
3	353			6	peach
+	703			238	green
♥	726			295	yellow
◒	762			234	lt grey
8	797			132	blue
−	970	−		316	orange

Design was stitched on a 7 1/2" x 7" piece of 14 count white Aida (design size 3" x 3 3/8"). Three strands of floss were used for Cross Stitch and 1 strand for Backstitch.

Shown on page 4.

SNOWBABY

X	DMC	1/4X	B'ST	ANC.	COLOR
☆	blanc	☆		2	white
■	310		/	403	black
▲	321			9046	red
3	353			6	peach
⁒	701			227	green
◒	762			234	lt grey
8	797			132	blue
−	970	−		316	orange
⬆	995			410	turquoise

Design was stitched on a 7" x 7 1/2" piece of 14 count white Aida (design size 3" x 3 3/8"). Three strands of floss were used for Cross Stitch and 1 strand for Backstitch.

Shown on page 4.

Stitch Count (41w x 46h)
14 count 3" x 3 3/8"
16 count 2 5/8" x 2 7/8"
18 count 2 3/8" x 2 5/8"

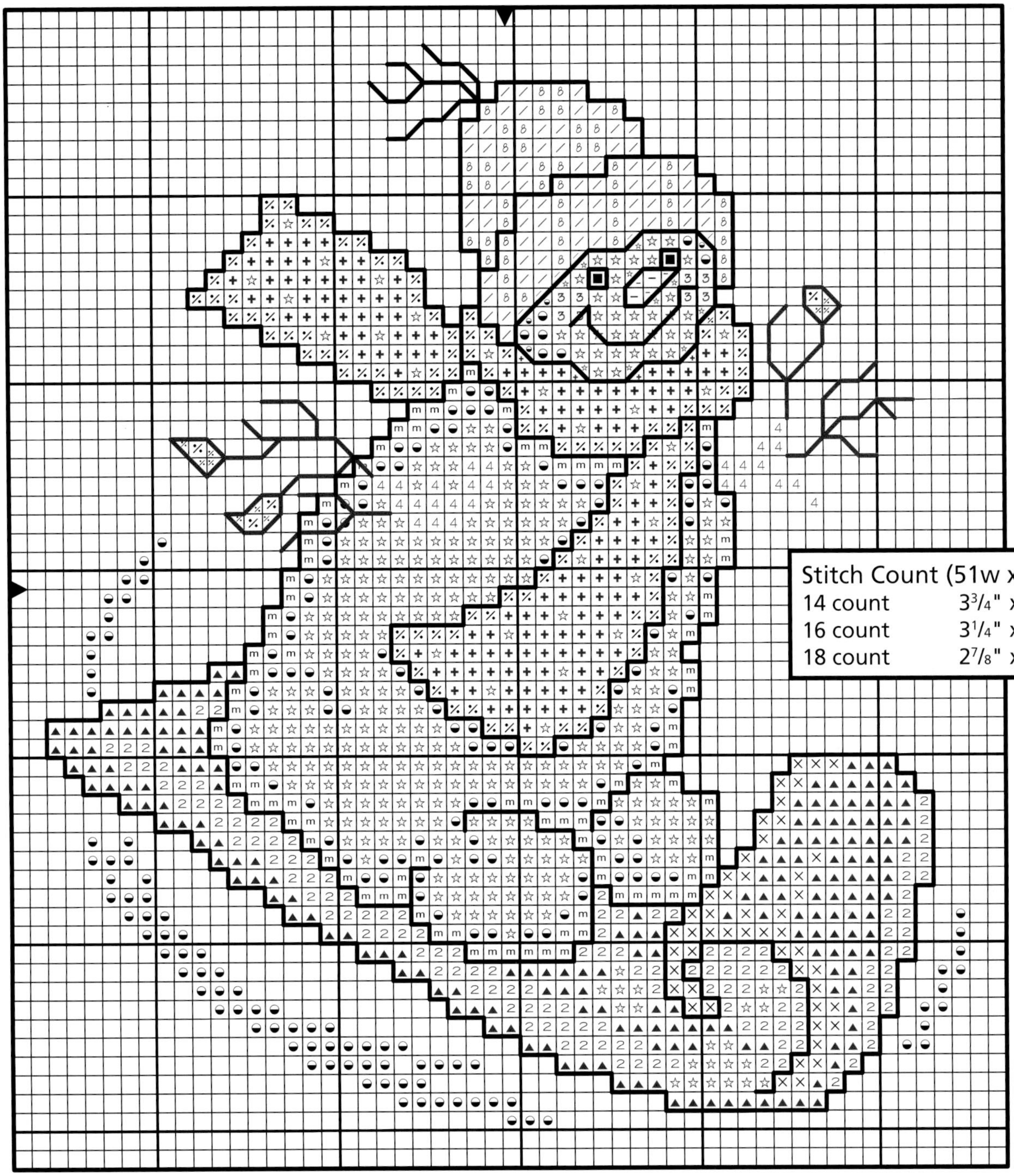

Stitch Count (51w x 58h)	
14 count	3 3/4" x 4 1/4"
16 count	3 1/4" x 3 5/8"
18 count	2 7/8" x 3 1/4"

SLEDDING SNOWMAN

X	DMC	1/4X	B'ST	ANC.	COLOR
☆	blanc	☆		2	white
■	310		/	403	black
m	318			399	grey
▲	321			9046	red
3	353			6	peach
4	433		/	358	brown
⁒	701	⁒		227	green
+	703	+		238	lt green
◒	762	◒		234	lt grey
8	797			132	blue
/	799	/		136	lt blue
2	816			1005	maroon
–	970	–		316	orange
☒	3705			35	melon

Design was stitched on an 8" x 8 1/2" piece of 14 count white Aida (design size 3 3/4" x 4 1/4"). Three strands of floss were used for Cross Stitch and 1 strand for Backstitch.

Shown on page 4.

ROLYPOLY SANTA

X	DMC	1/4X	B'ST	ANC.	COLOR
☆	blanc	☆		2	white
■	310		/	403	black
▲	321	▲		9046	red
★	352	★		9	peach
3	353	3		6	lt peach
+	703	+		238	green
=	726			295	yellow
◒	762	◒		234	lt grey
2	816	2		1005	maroon

Design was stitched on a $7\frac{1}{2}$" x $7\frac{1}{2}$" piece of 14 count white Aida (design size $3\frac{1}{8}$" x $3\frac{1}{2}$"). Three strands of floss were used for Cross Stitch and 1 strand for Backstitch. Design was also stitched on a $6\frac{1}{2}$" x 7" piece of 18 count white Aida (design size $2\frac{1}{2}$" x $2\frac{3}{4}$"). Two strands of floss were used for Cross Stitch and 1 strand for Backstitch. It was inserted in a $3\frac{1}{4}$" diameter gold-tone frame.

Shown on page 5 and back cover.

Stitch Count (43w x 49h)	
14 count	$3\frac{1}{8}$" x $3\frac{1}{2}$"
16 count	$2\frac{3}{4}$" x $3\frac{1}{8}$"
18 count	$2\frac{1}{2}$" x $2\frac{3}{4}$"

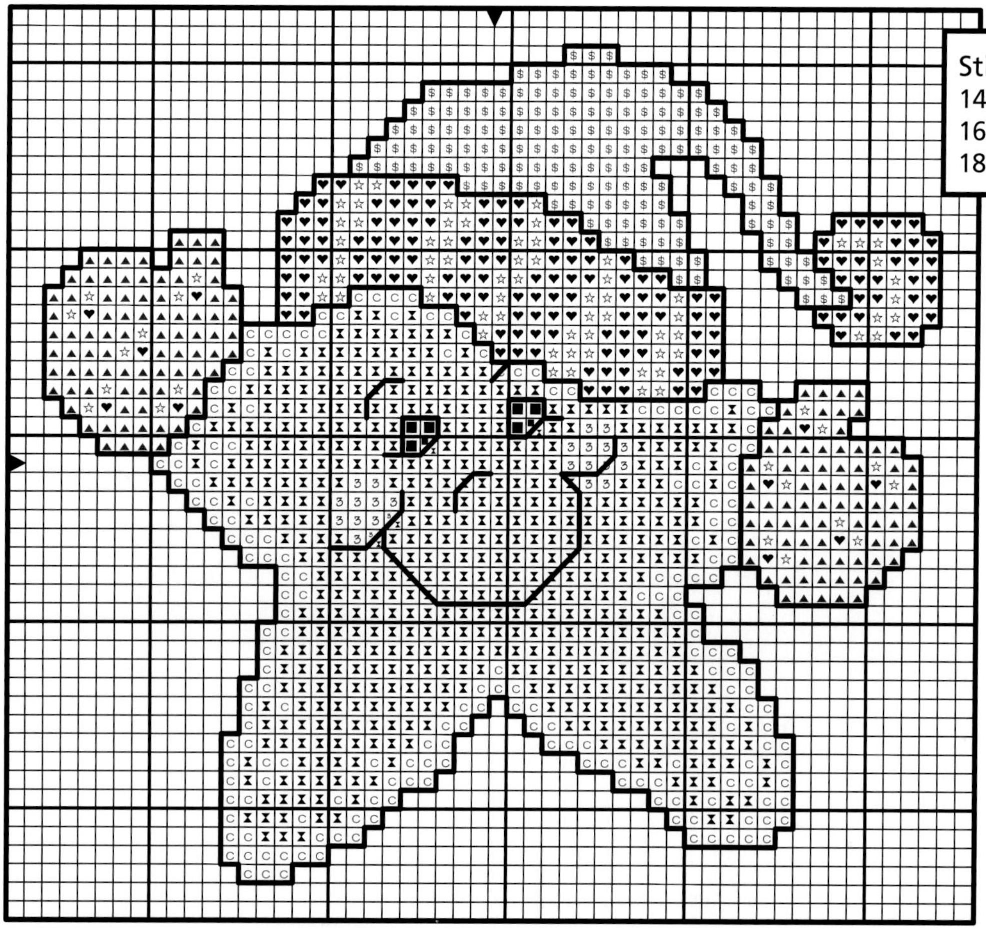

Stitch Count (50w x 45h)	
14 count	$3\frac{5}{8}$" x $3\frac{1}{4}$"
16 count	$3\frac{1}{8}$" x $2\frac{7}{8}$"
18 count	$2\frac{7}{8}$" x $2\frac{1}{2}$"

TWINKLE

X	DMC	1/4X	B'ST	ANC.	COLOR
☆	blanc			2	white
■	310	■	/	403	black
▲	321			9046	red
3	351	3		10	coral
$	699			923	green
♥	703			238	lt green
⧗	3078	⧗		292	lt yellow
c	3820			306	lt gold

Design was stitched on an 8" x $7\frac{1}{2}$" piece of 14 count white Aida (design size $3\frac{5}{8}$" x $3\frac{1}{4}$"). Three strands of floss were used for Cross Stitch and 1 strand for Backstitch.

Shown on page 4.

SKATING SNOWMAN

X	DMC	1/4X	B'ST	ANC.	COLOR
☆	blanc	☆		2	white
■	310		/	403	black
m	318			399	grey
3	353			6	peach
♥	433		/	358	brown
♦	554	♦		96	violet
⁒	701			227	green
+	703	+		238	lt green
◒	762	◒		234	lt grey
✖	797			132	blue
−	970	−		316	orange

Design was stitched on a $7^1/_2$" x $7^1/_2$" piece of 14 count white Aida (design size $3^3/_8$" x $3^1/_4$"). Three strands of floss were used for Cross Stitch and 1 strand for Backstitch.

Shown on page 4.

Stitch Count (46w x 45h)	
14 count	$3^3/_8$" x $3^1/_4$"
16 count	$2^7/_8$" x $2^7/_8$"
18 count	$2^5/_8$" x $2^1/_2$"

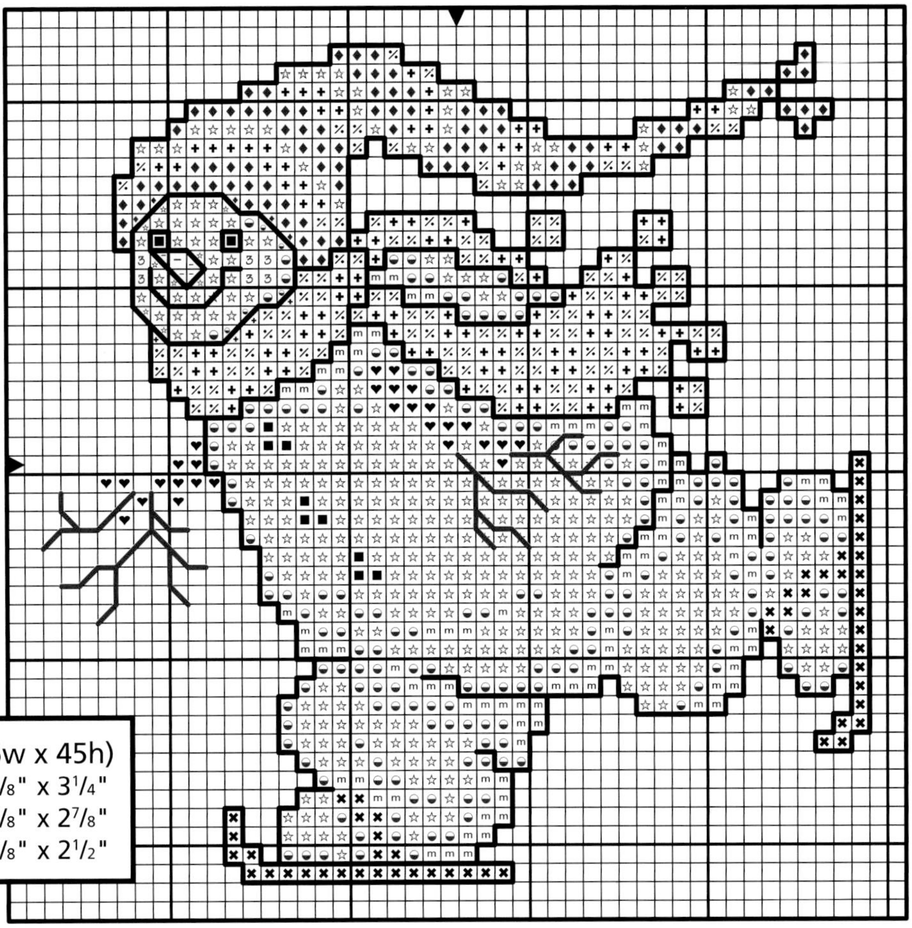

Stitch Count (48w x 44h)	
14 count	$3^1/_2$" x $3^1/_4$"
16 count	3" x $2^3/_4$"
18 count	$2^3/_4$" x $2^1/_2$"

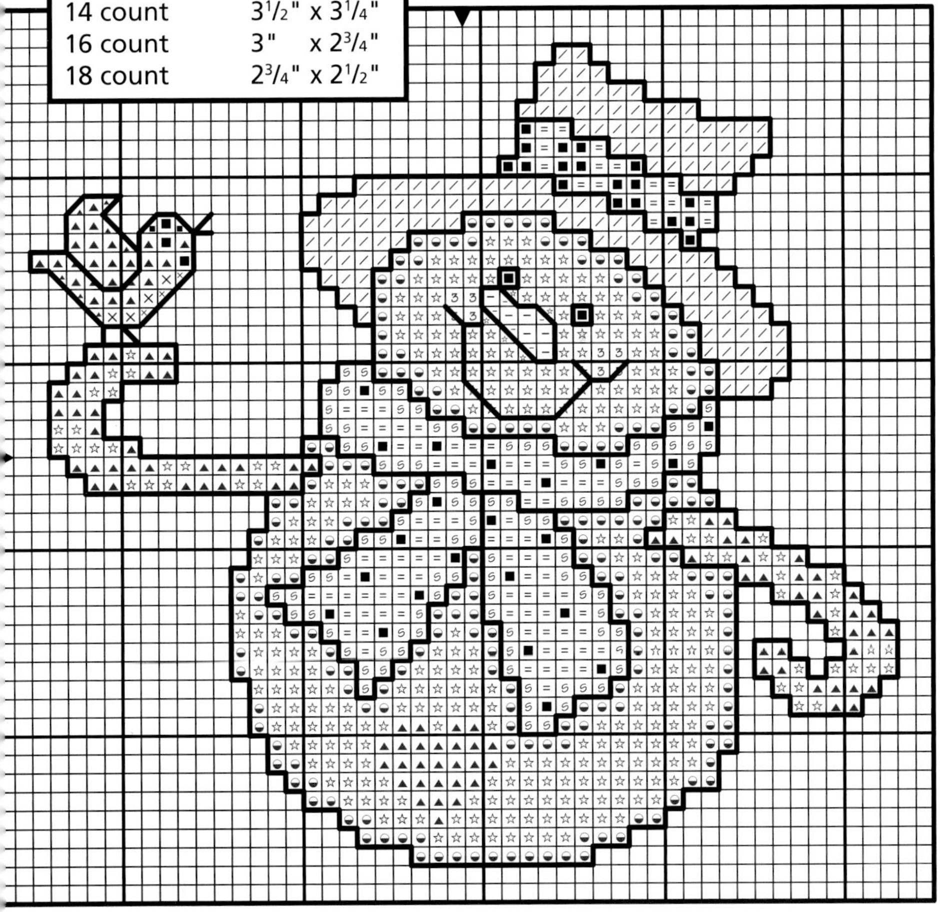

SNOWBABY WITH REDBIRD

X	DMC	1/4X	B'ST	ANC.	COLOR
☆	blanc	☆		2	white
■	310	■	/	403	black
▲	321	▲		9046	red
3	353			6	peach
=	726			295	yellow
S	729			890	gold
◒	762			234	lt grey
/	799			136	blue
−	970	−		316	orange
✕	3705	✕		35	melon

Design was stitched on a $7^1/_2$" x $7^1/_2$" piece of 14 count white Aida (design size $3^1/_2$" x $3^1/_4$"). Three strands of floss were used for Cross Stitch and 1 strand for Backstitch. Design was also stitched on a 7" x $6^1/_2$" piece of 18 count white Aida (design size $2^3/_4$" x $2^1/_2$"). Two strands of floss were used for Cross Stitch and 1 strand for Backstitch. It was inserted in a $3^1/_4$" diameter gold-tone frame.

Shown on page 4.

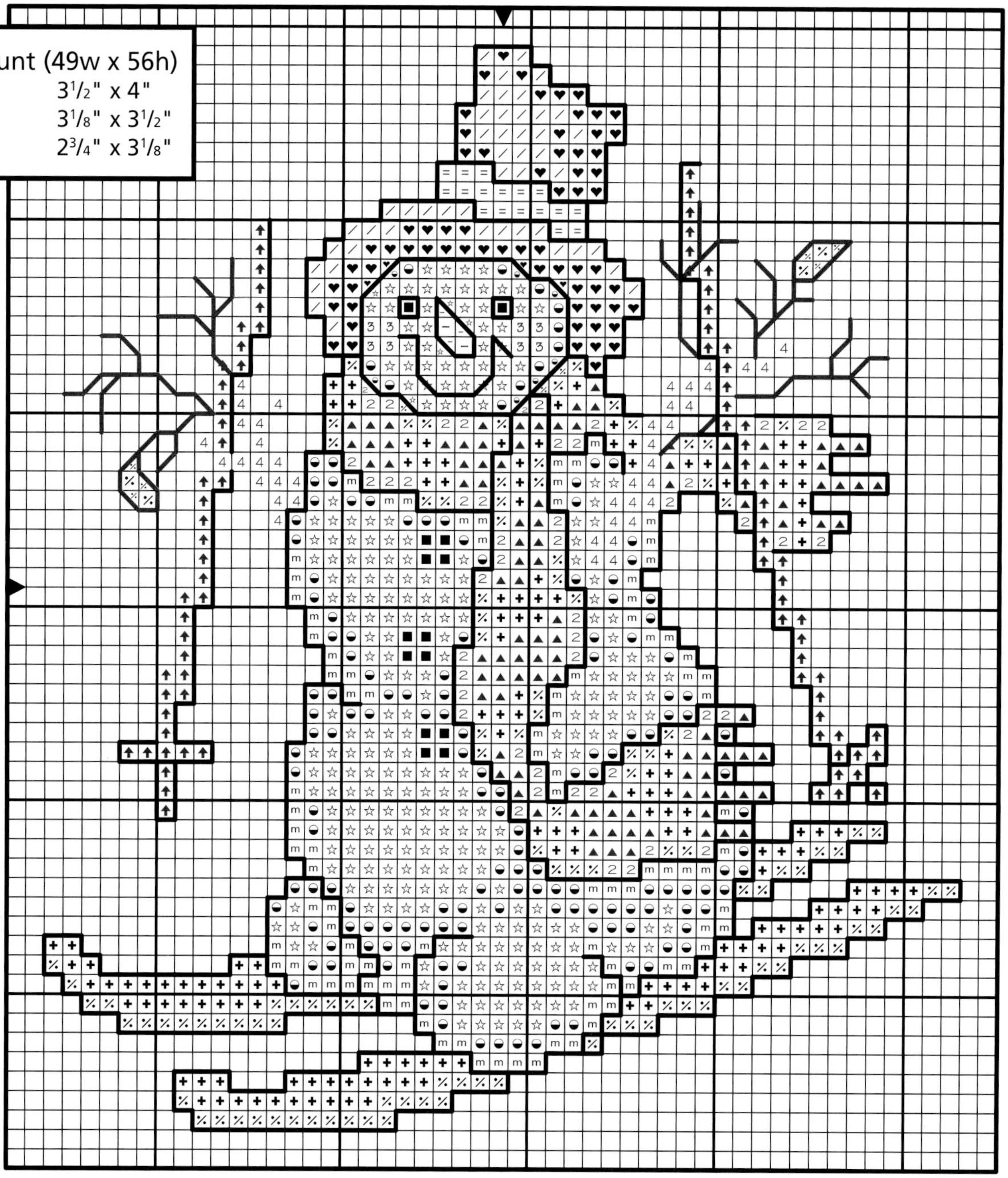

SKIING SNOWMAN

X	DMC	¼X	B'ST	ANC.	COLOR
☆	blanc	☆		2	white
■	310		/	403	black
m	318			399	grey
▲	321			9046	red
3	353			6	peach
4	433		/	358	brown
⁒	701	⁒		227	green
+	703			238	lt green

X	DMC	¼X	ANC.	COLOR
=	726		295	yellow
◒	762	◒	234	lt grey
♥	797	♥	132	blue
/	799		136	lt blue
2	816	2	1005	maroon
−	970	−	316	orange
⬆	995		410	turquoise

Design was stitched on a 7½" x 8" piece of 14 count white Aida (design size 3½" x 4"). Three strands of floss were used for Cross Stitch and 1 strand for Backstitch. Design was also stitched on a 7" x 7½" piece of 18 count white Aida (design size 2¾" x 3⅛"). Two strands of floss were used for Cross Stitch and 1 strand for Backstitch. It was inserted in a 3¼" diameter gold-tone frame.

Shown on page 4.

Stitch Count (56w x 52h)

14 count	4" x 3¾"
16 count	3½" x 3¼"
18 count	3⅛" x 3"

SNOW COUPLE

X	DMC	¼X	B'ST	ANC.	COLOR
☆	blanc	☆		2	white
■	310		/	403	black
m	318	m		399	grey
▲	321	▲		9046	red
3	353			6	peach
$	699			923	dk green
%	701	%		227	green
+	703			238	lt green

X	DMC	¼X	ANC.	COLOR
=	726	=	295	yellow
◒	762	◒	234	lt grey
8	797	8	132	blue
/	799	/	136	lt blue
–	970	–	316	orange
⧗	3078	⧗	292	lt yellow
×	3705		35	melon

Design was stitched on an 8" x 8" piece of 14 count white Aida (design size 4" x 3¾"). Three strands of floss were used for Cross Stitch and 1 strand for Backstitch.

Shown on page 4.

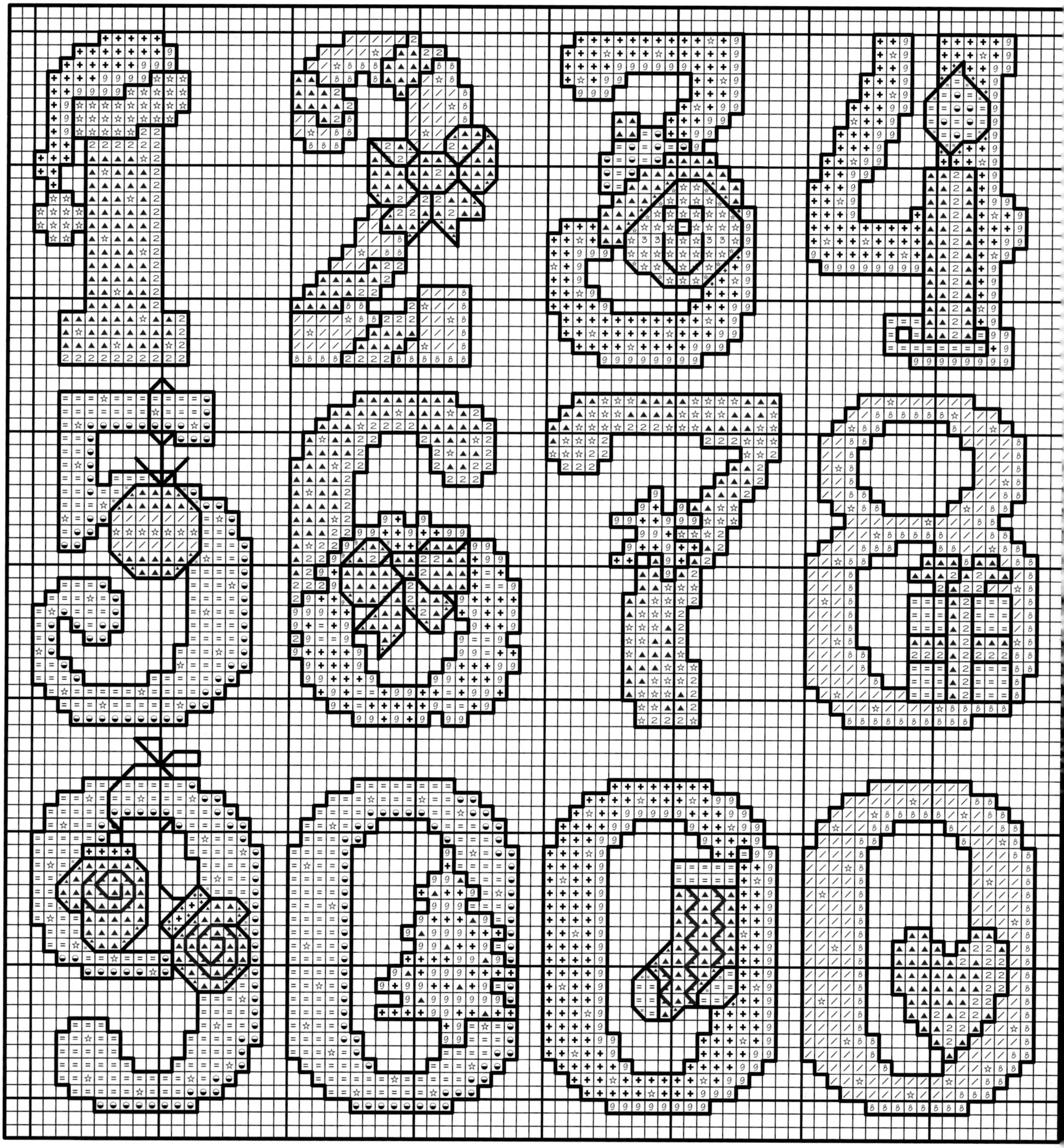

NUMBERS

X	DMC	1/4X	B'ST	ANC.	COLOR
☆	blanc	☆		2	white
	310		/	403	black
▲	321	▲		9046	red
3	353			6	peach
9	700	9		228	dk green
+	703	+		238	green
=	726	=	/	295	yellow
◒	729			890	gold
8	797			132	blue
/	799	/		136	lt blue
2	816			1005	maroon
−	970			316	orange

We used the numbers to stitch the holiday year on a 9" x 6" piece of 14 count white Aida (design size 5" x 1 7/8"). Three strands of floss were used for Cross Stitch and 1 strand for Backstitch.

Shown on page 3.

General Instructions

HOW TO READ CHARTS

Each chart is made up of a key and a gridded design on which each square represents a stitch. The symbols in the key tell which floss color to use for each stitch in the chart. The following headings and symbols are given:

X — Cross Stitch
DMC — DMC color number
$^1/_4$ X — Quarter Stitch
B'ST — Backstitch
ANC. — Anchor color number
COLOR — The name given to the floss color in these charts

A square filled with a symbol should be worked as a **Cross Stitch**.

A triangle with a reduced symbol should be worked as a **Quarter Stitch**.

A straight line should be worked as a **Backstitch**.

Sometimes the symbol for a **Cross Stitch** may be partially covered when a **Backstitch** crosses the square.

HOW TO STITCH

Always work **Cross Stitches** and **Quarter Stitches** first and then add the **Backstitch**. When stitching, bring the threaded needle up at **1** and all **odd** numbers and down at **2** and all **even** numbers.

Cross Stitch (X): For horizontal rows, work stitches in two journeys ***(Fig. 1)***. For vertical rows, complete each stitch as shown ***(Fig. 2)***.

Fig. 1

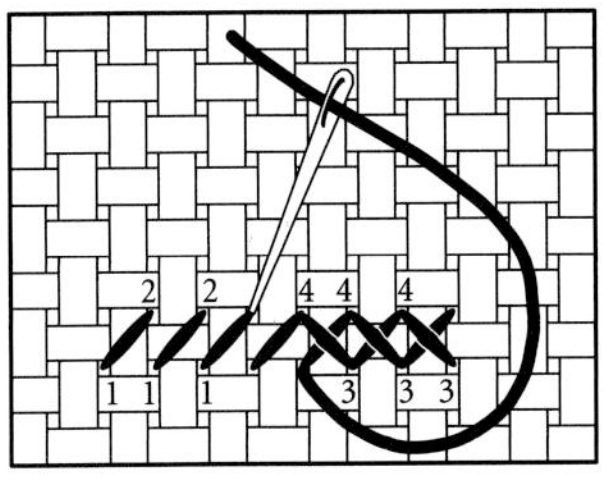

Fig. 2

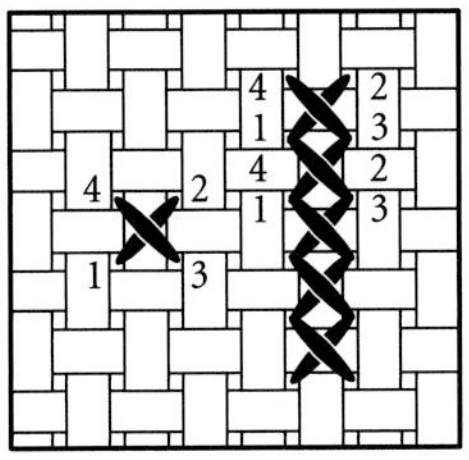

Quarter Stitch ($^1/_4$X): Come up at 1, and then split the fabric thread to go down at 2 ***(Fig. 3)***.

Fig. 3

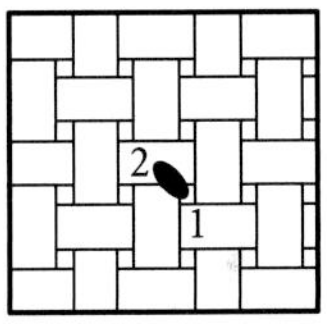

Backstitch (B'ST): For outlines and details, Backstitch should be worked after the design has been completed ***(Fig. 4)***.

Fig. 4

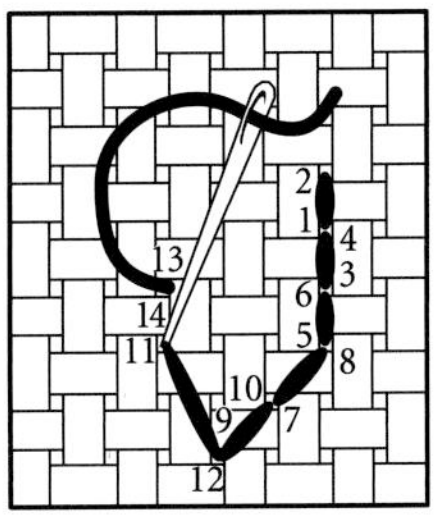

STITCHING TIPS

Preparing Fabric

Being sure to allow plenty of margin, cut the fabric to the desired size and overcast the raw edges. It is better to waste a little fabric than to come up short.

Working with Floss

To ensure smoother stitches, separate the floss strands and realign them before threading the needle. Keep stitching tension consistent. Begin and end the floss by running under several stitches on the back; never tie knots.

Where to Start

The horizontal and vertical center of each charted design is shown by arrows. You may start at any point on the charted design, but be sure the design will be centered on the fabric. Locate the center of the fabric by folding it in half, top to bottom and again left to right. On the charted design, count the number of squares (stitches) from the center of the chart to where you wish to start. Then, from the fabric's center, find your starting point by counting out the same number of fabric threads (stitches).

PROJECTS

Each design was stitched on 14 count white Aida using 3 strands of floss for Cross Stitch and 1 strand for Backstitch unless otherwise noted. Several of the designs were stitched on 18 count white Aida using 2 strands of floss for Cross Stitch and 1 strand for Backstitch unless otherwise noted.

Fabric provided courtesy of Charles Craft, Inc.
Embroidery floss provided courtesy of The DMC Corporation.

Production Team: Technical Writer – Mary Sullivan Hutcheson
Editorial Writer – Susan McManus Johnson
Senior Graphic Artist – Lora Puls
Graphic Artists – Dayle Carozza, Jacob Casleton, Dana Vaughn, and Janie Wright
Photo Stylist – Sondra Daniel
Photographer – Ken West

Instructions tested and photography models made by Gary Hutcheson, Phyllis Lundy, Donna Overman, Angie Perryman, and Anne Simpson.